Making Money Going into the Deal

Making Money Going into the Deal

The Art & Science of Real Estate

Second Edition

Thomas R. Stilp

This publication is designed to provide accurate and authoritative information in regard to the subject matter covered. It is sold with understanding that neither the author nor the publisher are engaged in rendering legal, accounting, or other professional services. If legal advice or other professional assistance is required, the services of a competent professional person should be sought.

—From a Declaration of Principles jointly adopted by a Committee of American Bar Association and a Committee of Publishers and Associations

Copyright © 2020 by Thomas R. Stilp.

Library of Congress Control Number:		2019942702
ISBN:	Hardcover	978-1-7960-3558-2
	Softcover	978-1-7960-3557-5
	eBook	978-1-7960-3556-8

All rights reserved. No part of this book may be reproduced or transmitted in any form or by any means, electronic or mechanical, including photocopying, recording, or by any information storage and retrieval system, without permission in writing from the copyright owner.

Print information available on the last page.

Rev. date: 01/02/2020

To order additional copies of this book, contact:
Xlibris
1-888-795-4274
www.Xlibris.com
Orders@Xlibris.com

CONTENTS

I. **INTRODUCTION** 9
   A. Why Buy Real Estate? 15
   B. Focus on Numerator (Income) Growth 21
   C. Be "On Top" of the Property 25

II. **DETERMINE WHAT THE PROPERTY IS WORTH** 27
   A. Finding the Right Property: The Initial Search 31
   B. Finding the Right Property: Anchoring of Price 34
   C. Price: Crunching the Numbers 37
      1. Capitalization Rate 38
      2. Net Operating Income 42

   D. Complex Analysis: Growth and Crunching the
      Numbers (Continued) 45
   E. Factors Influencing Growth in Cash Flows 51
   F. Qualitative Factors Influencing Price 54

III. **NEGOTIATION: CLOSING THE DEAL** 59
   A. Seller and Buyer Personalities 63
   B. Seller and Buyer Preferences 68
      1. Documents and People as Intermediaries 68
      2. The 3 Ps of Negotiating: Preferences, Priorities,
         and Preparation 74
      3. Seller Preferences: Decision Tree 77

   C. Integrative Negotiations 79
   D. Disorder in the Court 83

IV. THE PAPERWORK: PROFIT MAKING CLAUSES FOR THE BUYER 91
   A. Information Concerning the Income, Expenses and Cash Flow of the Property 97
      1. Document Inspection 97
      2. Seller Representations and Warranties Concerning Cash Flow and Leases 99

   B. Information Concerning the Condition of the Property 102
      1. Physical Inspection 102
      2. Seller Representations and Warranties Concerning Condition of Property 105

   C. Buyer Costs to Close the Transaction 111
   D. Buyer Remedies If Seller Fails to Perform or Has Given Incorrect Information 114
   E. The Whole Contract: Integrated Provisions 118
   F. Other Forms of Purchase: Alternative Financing 120
      1. Lease with Option to Buy 121
      2. Installment Sale Contract 122

   G. Forms of Ownership 128

V. CASE STUDY 133
   A. Forty-three-unit Apartment Building for $13,500 137
   B. The Use of Leverage 144
   C. Compounding 149

VI. IDEAS ABOUT RUNNING A PROPERTY 153
   A. Spreading Fixed Costs: Always Keep a Fully Rented Building 157
   B. Paying Your Management Company Right 162
   C. Getting Rid of Your Bad Tenants 167
      1. Rules of Thumb for Collection of Rent 167
      2. Evictions 169
      3. Screening Tenants 171
      4. Collecting Money Owed and Distress for Rent 172

    D. Keeping Your Good Tenants 175
       1. Securing Commitment.. 175
       2. Tenant Questionnaires... 178
       3. Impact Matrix: Threats and Opportunities2 181

VII. CONCLUSION.. 187

APPENDIX 191
SAMPLE RIDER TO REAL ESTATE CONTRACT 193
SAMPLE TENANT APPLICATION 207
CASE STUDY MATERIALS 211
IMPACT MATRIX 231

I

INTRODUCTION

A successful investor buys large properties not by luck but through learned skills that depend on the conscientious application of certain techniques. In some books, instruction on how to make friends while negotiating a "win-win" deal excels with advice on people skills but is short on quantitative analysis. At some point, a buyer has to know how to handle numbers. Income-producing real estate is, after all, an investment with financial assumptions concerning income, risks, and rewards. On the other hand, advice about the numbers in other books generally assumes a postgraduate degree in finance, statistics, and accounting but is short on people skills necessary to close a deal.

A buyer needs one practical source to understand people skills while at the same time, learn the quantitative side of the business. An optimist says the glass is half full, a pessimist says the glass is half empty, but the realist says you've got twice as much glass as you need. Realistic, practical information—that is what we hope to accomplish with this book.

Much has been written about real estate for broad appeal—real estate investors, developers, bankers, tenants, salespeople, mortgage brokers, lawyers, accountants, tax advisors, property managers, sellers, and buyers. A number of books tell an investor where to look for properties, but not whether the property is truly valuable, or the A through Z steps to successfully negotiate and buy the property. This book is specifically written for one real estate investor: the buyer. No other book captures the buyer's point of view, with the strategies and techniques necessary to become a successful buyer and make money.

Organized in six general areas, this book follows an actual transaction the way in which events happened. Although the focus is on a residential apartment building, in fact, many principals discussed are equally applicable to all property types.

The book should be read from beginning to end. Later, those chapters with specific calculations may be used as a reference.

- *Introduction.* The introductory part of this book discusses the attraction of real estate as an investment vehicle, income growth, and good decision making for profit.
- *Determine What the Property is Worth.* The second part of this book explains how to find the right property and determine what that property is really worth.
- *Negotiation and Closing the Deal.* Third, this book reviews the art of negotiation, letters of intent, intermediaries, and how to close a deal on terms favorable to the buyer.
- *The Paperwork: Profit Making Clauses for the Buyer.* The fourth part of this book describes how to put negotiation onto paper in a real estate contract with profit making clauses for the buyer and compares various forms of property ownership.
- *Case Study.* Fifth, a case study autopsies the purchase of a forty-three-unit building using as little as $13,500, with the techniques discussed in prior sections of the book, and reproduces the actual documents and letters used to buy the property.
- *Ideas About Running a Property.* The final part of this book assumes the right property has been purchased and explains how to operate the property, maximize collections, rid the property of nonpaying tenants and keep good tenants as long as possible.

Making good decisions about real estate can be learned. It is said a wise person learns from experience, but the wisest learns from the experience of others. Known as modeling, copying the strategy of others may be a faster and more effective way to learn than the school of hard knocks. And reading about how to purchase properties is a low cost, low risk way to learn from the experience of others.

But the buyer should not stop there. The buyer should take the experience learned here and make it their own. Experience is not what happens to you; it is what you do with what happens to you. To paraphrase Mark Twain, be careful to get out of experience only what you are told and stop there, lest you be like the cat that sits down on a hot stove lid. The cat will never sit down on a hot lid again, but it will never sit down on a cold one either.

A

Why Buy Real Estate?

Will Rogers said, "Buy land! They ain't making any more of it." That admonition may be part of every person's motivation to own real estate. Real estate ownership is founded on the belief each piece of real estate is unique. More than just an investment, real estate is a tangible manifestation of an investor's worth—ideas that can be seen and felt in the dirt, bricks and mortar of the property.

People are motivated to own property by several needs. People need shelter. Residential real estate has a fundamental value: everyone must live somewhere. Looking more long term, as a store of economic value, real estate functions as the nest egg for retirement savings. For others, property ownership is motivated by financial speculation, buying, and selling for the highest profit. For others still, real estate offers psychological benefits, a need for security, being rooted in a particular neighborhood, social status, or participation in the ingrained "American Dream." The strength of real estate was recognized during this country's worst depression, when President Franklin Delano Roosevelt said, "Real estate cannot be lost or stolen, nor can it be carried away. Managed with reasonable care, it is about the safest investment in the world."[1]

Most of us know it is better to get a 10% rate of return rather than 3.5%, but beyond the general concept, few of us actually think of how much we'll have if we make different investments. For purposes of illustration, assume a long investment period in which we invest $1 at the end of each month for sixty-six years.

Under mattress	-0-%	$ 792.00 (66 years x 12 months x $1)
Money Market	3.5%	$ 3,099.64
U.S. Treasuries	5.0%	$ 6,222.57
Stocks	10%	$ 85,711.69
Real Estate / Business	20%	$ 29,079,663.65

Imagine instead of $1, the amount invested was $100. The return on investment in real estate would increase to $2.9 billion. (Calculations are based on the frequently used formula for future worth of $1 per period $(1+i/12)^{(t*12)}-1/(i/12)$ discussed in the Case Study in Part V where "i" is the rate of return and "t" is the time in years.)

No doubt many investors make money in the stock market, but given the efficient market theory, ordinarily an investor cannot make above average profits (say above 7%) for any extended time. Real estate, however, is *not* typically an efficient market and provides pockets of profit opportunities that experienced real estate purchasers find.

Considering the buy-and-hold-for-return strategies of stocks versus real estate, proponents of stock investing argue that real estate should have higher returns because real estate is illiquid (that is, an investor can't get their money out). Investors in real estate, they argue, should be paid an "illiquidity premium" to compensate investors with a higher return for their general inability to withdraw funds from the investment. The concept of an "illiquidity premium" is where the theory of stock investing, which recognizes that real estate should pay a premium for lack of liquidity, clashes with the practice of stock investing in at least two respects. First, a good real estate investment will pay its investors with quarterly or even monthly cash flow. Given the diminution of dividend payments, many stocks no longer distribute regular cash payments to investors. In this respect, stocks have become more illiquid than real estate. Second, as the result of severe market value fluctuations, professional stock analysts advise investors now to "hold" stock for the long term to allow stock values to return. A long-term hold has resulted in stocks having a de facto status of illiquidity, but without the premium for higher returns to investors already recognized as necessary in real estate.

The way an investment is located presents another myth in the comparison of stock and real estate investing. Many professional stock analysts claim to specialize in locating that hidden gem, finding value in "undervalued common stocks." Again, in theory, the search for the undervalued stock sounds fine but is unlikely in practice. Stocks operate in a highly efficient market where information is electronically and systematically transmitted to many people simultaneously. Thus, barring the use of inside information (which is illegal), what one professional analyst knows is generally known to many others. (Analysts will claim the difference lies in the interpretation of the information by each analyst, but then you are betting on the jockey and not the horse.) Through well-established networks of intermediaries, professional analysts enjoy almost instantaneous globalization of information.

The Efficient Markets Hypothesis holds an investor can *not* earn an abnormally high return in the stock market because stock prices reflect all available information; competition among investors guarantees stocks are properly priced in the market, and the market provides a set of efficient arrangements where buyers and sellers are brought together through the price mechanism.

Real estate, on the other hand, is characterized by inefficient markets, idiosyncratic knowledge known only to a few people, and localization of product. Use of inside information is not only legal but is encouraged. A net cast in a search for "undervalued" real estate is far more likely to result in a catch than in the stock market. Good investors not only find profitable real estate (often real estate is not publicly available, a common fact in our investments), but also operate the real estate efficiently to return consistent cash flows to investors. Unlike the stock market where thousands may ride a wave of short-term profits, in real estate, success is highly individual.

For those in the real estate business, using the acronym, "why investors 'LYC' (like) real estate," recalls the three advantages real estate investors look for: Leverage, Yield, and Control.

Leverage: Leverage means an investor gets more than a dollar's worth of property for each dollar put up to buy the real estate. With 90% leverage on a $100,000 property, the investor puts down only $10,000 to own a property worth ten times that amount.

Yield: A real estate investor realizes yield in any of four ways, which may be defined by another acronym: Buying real estate is a great "IDEA," because through real estate, the investor gets Income, Depreciation, Equity, and Appreciation.

I: Income: One attribute of an income-producing property is that the rents, laundry machines, parking, and miscellaneous fees generate income. Income is part of the investor's yield.

D: Depreciation: The real estate investor is entitled to shelter income generated from the property through depreciation. Depreciation recognizes that over time, a property deteriorates, suffering from curable and, in some cases, incurable, obsolescence. A government subsidy in the form of a tax break, depreciation was designed to provide incentives to property owners to make capital improvements on their property. Although designed to recognize physical deterioration of a property, depreciation is largely a paper loss. In reality, depreciation may have little effect on a property's actual value. The IRS (Internal Revenue Service) allows depreciation to be treated as an actual expense even though no money was spent. On an apartment building, depreciation may be taken over a period of 27.5 years, or 3.63% of the value of the building each year. Thus, if the owner's basis (akin to cost) on the building is $100,000, the owner is entitled to a depreciation deduction against the building's income in the amount of $100,000 x 3.63%, or $3,630 per year. Depreciation may only be taken against the capital improvements, such as the building itself, and not the land under the building. According to the IRS, land cannot depreciate because it lasts forever.

Depreciation is ordinarily a deferral of taxes, not a permanent write-off. The IRS will keep track of the depreciation deductions on the property owner's annual tax returns, so in two years, the $100,000 property is worth $100,000-$3,630-$3,630—or $92,740. If the property was originally purchased for $100,000 (to keep it straightforward, assuming little to no land value) and is sold two years later for $110,000, the IRS requires the owner to recognize a profit of $17,260 ($110,000-$92,740), not simply $10,000 from the original purchase.

Still, depreciation gives the investor two savings: (1) the investor may defer payment of taxes until the property is sold, which may occur years in the future, and (2) the investor enjoys a tax savings by converting rental income, which is taxed at the higher *ordinary gain* rate (e.g., 30%) to income from capital gains (the sale proceeds), which is taxed at the lower *capital gains* rate (e.g., 15%). Given the time discrepancy from operation to point of sale, rental income is sheltered from taxes through offsetting depreciation deductions. There truly is a savings to the investor through depreciation, increasing the investor's overall yield.

E: Equity: Equity buildup also affects yield. Equity buildup occurs the longer the investor holds on to the property and pays down the mortgage. Over time, that part of the monthly mortgage payment toward principal increases as the payment towards interest decreases.

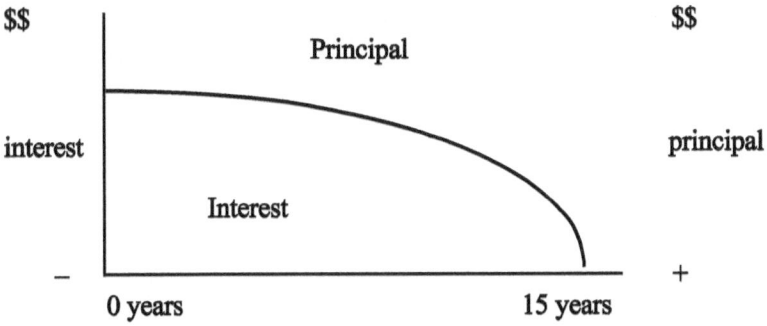

A loan with a fifteen-year amortization schedule is fully paid in fifteen years. By the way, the term *amortization* is derived from Latin, meaning "to kill off," which is what happens to the loan over time.

A: Appreciation: Appreciation also affects yield. Each year the investor owns the real estate, the property may increase in value. Some investors do not estimate appreciation as part of their return. It depends on too many factors they cannot control; if they get appreciation, they take it as a bonus.

Buying real estate is a great "IDEA," as Income, Depreciation, Equity buildup, and Appreciation all affect yield on real estate unlike on any other type of asset.

Control: Control is the final reason "why investors 'LYC' real estate." A property owner has control over the real estate investment by making decisions that will affect the building. An investor who purchases one thousand shares of stock in a publicly traded company does not have control over the company. The investor cannot control a stock price no matter how hard the investor tries. A property owner, however, may increase rents, undertake capital improvements, or sell the property, and in these ways, exercise control.

B

Focus on Numerator (Income) Growth

While talking about "why investors 'LYC' real estate" and why buying real estate is a great "IDEA" for yield, apartment buildings are not just about profits. Real estate is for people, not just for profits. A property owner is really selling a product to the people: three-dimensional space over time.[2]

The profitability of this three-dimensional space depends on whether the owner focuses on growing the property's income or cutting the property's expenses. For reasons discussed below, the successful owner focuses on growing income.

For purposes of this discussion, the profit a property generates depends on two factors: (1) income, how much the property owner brings in, and (2) expenses, how much the property owner pays out. What is left over may be loosely defined as "profit." The profitability (Π) of a property may be measured by the simple ratio of income divided by expenses:

$$\Pi = \frac{\text{INCOME}}{\text{EXPENSES}}$$

A property that brings in as much as it pays out has a profitability ratio of 1:1-$1 made for every $1 spent. A property that has a profitability ratio of 1.3:1

means $1.30 for every $1 spent, resulting in a 30¢ premium. Conversely, a ratio of .75:1 means for every 75¢ earned, it costs the property owner $1, a losing proposition. Thus, increasing the numerator (income) improves the profitability ratio; similarly, decreasing the denominator (expenses) while the numerator remains the same will enhance the profitability ratio.

Although a property owner seeks to minimize expenses, a property may perform poorly if the owner focuses on cutting expenses (denominator cuts). An owner will not achieve long-term profitability when denominator cuts reduce services to tenants and short-change maintenance so that the building deteriorates. After initiating cuts in services, an owner cannot understand why rents stagnate. Rather than denominator (expense) cuts, the property owner should focus on numerator (income) growth and increase revenue by creating more value for tenants.

Leverage-based efficiency gains come from raising the numerator in productivity ratios (revenue and net profits) rather than from reducing the denominator (costs). The goal is to increase the bang for a given buck rather than the other way around, reducing the buck (costs) for a given bang (revenue).[3]

Creating value for tenants begins with a sense of mission and an ordering of priorities. An inverse pyramid should reflect the owner's priorities:

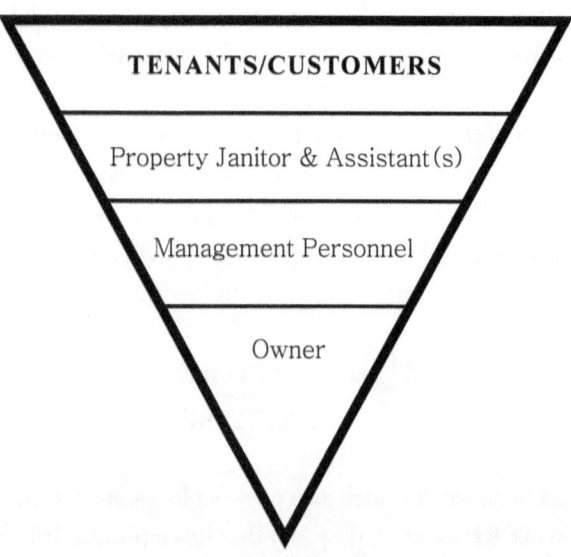

Tenants are customers. Tenants are more willing to pay rent if they perceive value. So too the people who are on the front line, dealing with tenants day-to-day, are important for the success of the building.

A cut in expenses, such as deferred maintenance, has a ripple effect. Management is told to cut back on expenses and allows part of the building to deteriorate. Over time, the people who work on the building see the property suffer from deferred maintenance. Tenants notice the building deteriorate, and the building cannot attract higher rents. This concatenation of events can only lead to further problems.

The ripple effect will be negative with denominator (expense) cuts. On the other hand, with numerator (income) growth, the effect can be positive, seen in the service-profit chain:

SERVICE-PROFIT RIPPLE EFFECT

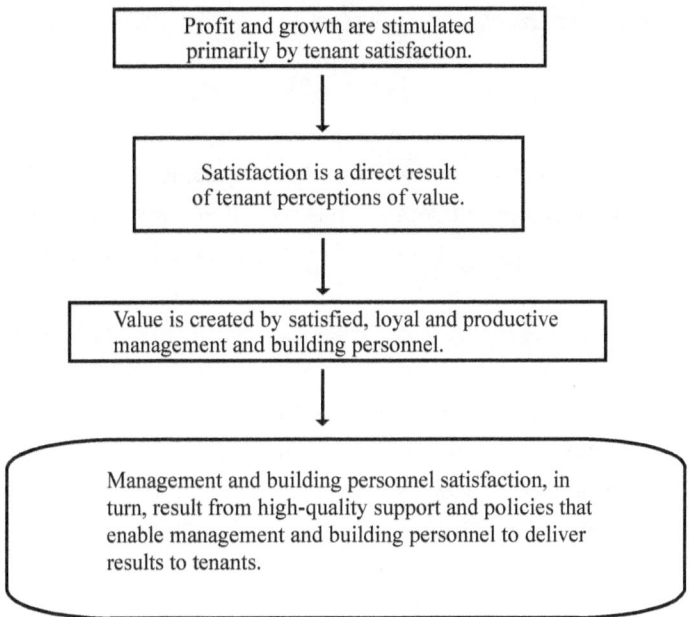

Denominator cuts may improve profitability in the short run, but a good reputation and an attractive building create long-term value.

A focus on revenue growth is not as difficult as it may first appear. Revenue growth begins with a fundamental reason for owning property beyond just making money. In fact, a real estate investor may make money without focusing on it. Consider having a mission statement. The mission statement accomplishes two purposes. First, the mission statement gives guidance to the people who work with the property; the mission statement allows individuals who work together to share a set of expectations about their work, creating collective values and behavioral norms that serve a control function. The mission statement sets forth an ideology, and people know steps are to be taken that are consistent with the mission statement. Second, by publicly espousing a point of view, people working with the property become more likely to behave consistently with that point of view. Individuals will align their goals and behaviors to those of the real estate mission.

Take for example this mission statement used by a successful real estate company in Chicago, Illinois:

> "TO IMPROVE THE PROPERTIES WE OWN, AND TO PROVIDE GOOD HOUSING AT AN AFFORDABLE COST FOR AS MANY PEOPLE AS POSSIBLE."

The mission statement does not even mention making money. Instead, the mission statement focuses on the idea that "housing is for people." More than a nice-sounding platitude, the mission statement forms the operating philosophy of the company that can be broken down into two parts:

- "To improve the properties we own": The company undertakes major capital improvements with each property. Capital improvements become part of the operating budget. By improving the property, the company addresses reputational concerns in the community and, as a result, consistently sees revenue growth. Tenants perceive value and are willing to pay higher rents. In addition, capital improvements maintain the integrity of the building and ensure appreciation upon resale of the property at a later date.
- "At an affordable cost for as many people as possible": The company's mission is to provide housing for as many people as possible. Thus, the company has an aggressive acquisition objective, a volume business with attention focused on the company's core competency—the housing market. With a reputation for having good properties, revenues grow.

C

Be "On Top" of the Property

Facilitating the mission statement means the real estate investor should be "on top" of the property. To be on top of the property, the investor needs information. Information must be timely to allow early corrective action in managing the property in areas that impact income. One of the best ways to be "on top" of the property is to visit the property regularly. Although this point seems transparent, it is easily overlooked by property owners in the throes of month-to-month operating statements and tenant problems.

Information "transfer costs"—defined as (1) inaccurate information from others, (2) difficulty in monitoring information others provide, and (3) verification of detail—increase (become more costly) as an investor's knowledge about a property moves from the specific to the general, and the investor knows less and less about the property. The costs of transferring specific knowledge affecting the property's performance increase the further the owner is removed from the property. The person on the spot, with idiosyncratic knowledge, is more likely to know if a particular repair is needed, has been performed, or if a problem reoccurs. By the time the information is transferred to the owner, the opportunity to act may be lost:

The costs of transferring knowledge moves on a continuum:

General Knowledge ⟶ Specific Knowledge

The investor wants to make decisions at the specific knowledge level. With only general knowledge, the investor will feel less secure and unwilling (or unable) to make difficult decisions when the future of the property is at stake. An out-of-control property, with bad tenants and deferred maintenance, is frequently the result of an absentee owner who has only general knowledge about the property.

The owner has the greatest incentive to use information productively. The owner must be involved in choosing alternatives to operate the property. By visiting the buildings, the investor minimizes the cost of getting information and increases the likelihood of making good decisions.

End Notes

1. A. D. Kessler, *A Fortune At Your Feet*, pp. xviii (1994).
2. J. Graaskamp, *Graaskamp on Real Estate*, Urban Land Institute, (Stephen Jarchow editor, 1991), pp. xiii and 314.
3. G. Hamel and C.K. Prahalad, *Competing for the Future*, pp. 173-81, Harvard Business School Press, Boston, MA (1996).

II

DETERMINE WHAT THE PROPERTY IS WORTH

A good place to find apartment buildings is the Internet or classified section of the local newspaper. At least that was back in the day for the first edition of this book. Since then, the Internet has become the major source of information. Regardless, in a major metropolitan area, there are literally dozens of buildings for sale each week. Consider these ads taken at random from the *Chicago Tribune*, real estate section, classified ads, or as may appear on the internet (with pictures and information):

> "13 UNIT BRICK w/ Huge Apts 4C gar, Owner Financ-Assum Mortg 15% dwn $429K"

or

> "40-U, 32-U & 18-Units
> • ** TAKE OVER DEBT ***
> • Owner fin."

Although the dollar amounts may change over time and with different properties and in different markets, the methods described here for purchasing may be applied over and over. How to determine what a property is really worth will be the subject of the next sections, which include the following:

(A) How to find the right property
(B) What effect list price has on anchoring the purchase price

(C) How to calculate what a property is really worth using simple analysis
(D) When to use a more complex analysis
(E) How to determine growth in cash flows
(F) What qualitative factors influence price

We discuss each in turn.

A

Finding the Right Property: The Initial Search

Finding the right property will depend on screening buildings that fit the investor profile from those that do not. In the initial phone call, five questions may help the investor narrow the search:

1. "What is the condition of the property?" Some problems may put the property outside the investor's criteria, for example, buildings in need of large capital improvements or repairs that may require different expertise than the investor can bring to the property.

2. "How many units are vacant?" A 15%-25% vacancy reflects a mildly distressed property. If the vacancy is a result of the building's location in an undesirable neighborhood (known as external obsolescence, which is generally incurable), there may not be much an investor can do. If the vacancy is the result of poor management by current ownership, however, the investor may add value through better management.

3. "Why is the owner selling?" An owner near retirement may simply want out of the property and be willing to finance part or all of the price. Sometimes it is the owner who is distressed and not the

property. An out-of-state owner may be flexible on terms. An owner that is both out of state and retired (the "Florida factor," for those moving from a colder climate who might retire to Florida) may be extremely flexible, provided the current owner has reasonable assurances of trouble-free payments.

4. "Is the seller motivated? Is the seller willing to hold paper, such as 10% of the purchase price if the seller gets a reasonable price?" The answer to question number 3 will suggest the seller's flexibility, and this question number 4 asks it directly. Here, the buyer explores the amount of seller financing. If the seller is not willing to hold 10%, will the seller consider 7% or 8%? Price is not an issue because the question offered a reasonable price, contradicting the possibility, at least initially, of a lowball offer. If there is no seller financing, move on to another property, unless there are unique features about this property the investor wants.

5. "Is there anything else about the property?" This open-ended question allows the seller, or the broker, to tell the investor positive information about the property. For example, the property may be near a park, recreation area, public transit, or a new development that will increase demand for housing in the immediate neighborhood. Asking an open-ended question may also reveal whether there are any *other* offers on the property. Multiple offers on a property allow the seller to play one buyer off the other and can only benefit the seller through a bidding war. If the property is really attractive, the investor may submit a "backup offer," asking the seller, or the seller's broker, to put the offer in their back pocket if the first offer falls through.

You may want to write the five questions above on a card to be sure each question is asked during a phone call. If the seller balks at any of the questions, simply say, "I am trying to understand what you are looking for so we can make an offer to meet both our needs and not waste your time or mine." Obviously, the deal must work for both parties, and both have to pull the rope in the same direction to get the deal done.

After searching for properties in the newspaper or Internet and asking questions over the phone, you will have a better idea which properties meet your criteria. Next, screen properties by price.

Suppose a particular property is worth $100,000 to you. If its asking price is $80,000, you would buy it because (from your perspective) the property's perceived benefit ($100,000) exceeds its cost. In making the purchase, you make yourself better off. You have given up $80,000 to receive something more valuable—a property whose benefit is worth $100,000. But how do you know a property is worth $100,000? The effects of anchoring of price on the buying decision and determining what a property is really worth are the subjects of the next sections.

B

Finding the Right Property: Anchoring of Price

The importance of determining value of a property is critical to a sound investment decision. The investor makes money going into the deal. A sure way to get into debt hell is to overpay for a property. Once in, the investor may be stuck with a poorly performing property. Real estate is illiquid and cannot be readily sold and converted to cash. Having overpaid for the property, an investor will feel the effects of a poor decision in the monthly debt service on the building and ultimately, the profit (or loss) when the building is sold. When in doubt, the investor may remember Mark Twain's advice: It is always easier to stay out than it is to get out.

How does the investor determine if the asking price is justified? Though not determinative of a property's worth, asking price has a powerful influence on buying decisions because of the phenomenon of "anchoring." Anchoring is a decision heuristic, a shortcut or rule of thumb that implicitly directs a buyer's judgment to a predetermined price, i.e., the asking price. Generally, heuristics serve as a mechanism for coping with complex decisions, like how to determine the price of a property. Heuristics may be helpful but, like many shortcuts, can lead to serious decision errors.

In real estate, anchoring affects buying decisions. Anchoring of price is prevalent in the real estate industry where sellers and brokers attempt to get and keep the highest price possible for a property. Having set a price, as a result of seller and buyer expectations created by anchoring, it seems the actual sale price usually must come within a certain range of the asking price if a sale is to occur. Although most sales occur this way, it does not mean the investor should buy property this way and simply assume the asking price approximates the property's actual worth.

It is a hard fact of real estate that the asking price often has very little to do with actual value of the property. What the seller has paid and invested in the property will be the seller's value. But actual value is the price *someone else* is willing to pay for that property.

Why can't the investor depend on the asking price? The asking price of a property would be useful if real estate were an efficient market. The asking price for other assets—such as automobiles, stocks, bonds, or clothing—can be tested by an efficient market. These assets are bought and sold with regular frequency. The efficient market presupposes a free exchange of information and *many sales* of the *same asset* in an arm's length transaction between a willing seller and buyer not under compulsion to sell or buy. The stock market is an example of an efficient market. Thousands of shares of General Motors stock are traded daily at a price known to anyone who looks in the paper or on the Internet.

In an efficient market, the list price of a property would reflect the property's fair market value. But the real estate market lacks publicly available information about properties; for example, a property's income, expenses, vacancies, and capital improvements are not public information. Even if information were available to the investor, it is not reported or audited or under strict government scrutiny as other markets are supposed to be. The accuracy and amount of information aside, any information gathered by the real estate investor, even if available, is of limited value. Each piece of real estate is unique, and income and expenses for one property are not readily transferable to another property with any great accuracy. Assuming very similar properties existed, information may be stale and sales may be weeks or months apart and not reflective of current property values.

As can be seen, asking price is not determinative of a property's true worth because real estate is not an efficient market. The list price of a property presumably reflects fair market value, but the reality is very different. The asking price is really nothing more than what the seller *wants* for the property.

Instead of using the asking price, a buyer of income-producing property has another criterion to judge the value of a property: the income of the property itself. The income of a property provides an objective measure of that property's worth to the investor. Using an objective measure of value available beforehand—before the price of the property is agreed upon and the contract signed—minimizes the effects of anchoring. The buyer should be open to disconfirming information, questioning the list price, and readjusting the price consistent with the more objective criteria using the income of the property. The buyer always should ask, "Does this price make sense?" in light of a priori measures of the property's worth given by its income.

C

Price: Crunching the Numbers

What is a building worth? In answering that question, it is useful to remember the investor is not buying real estate, but a set of financial assumptions, an idea best said by University of Wisconsin real estate professor, James Graaskamp:

> "There is a mystique to the ownership of land and a misleading permanence to brick and mortar which motivate investors in real estate enterprises to their disadvantage . . . However, the product of real estate is not to be confused with the business of real estate. The business of real estate is a cash-cycle business, going from money in the bank to goods-in process (construction) to inventory (property management) back to cash . . . When investing in a bond, it is possible to know the cost and date of acquisition, the amount and date of the interest coupon, and the amount and date of repayment if the bond is called or matures. All the elements for determining yield on a bond are fixed by contract and transaction documents. In real estate almost none of the elements necessary to forecast yield and risk are provided by the nature of the transaction, and it is necessary to supply these elements by assumption . . . If you can't 'buy' the assumptions as presented, you cannot afford the real estate product about which those assumptions were made, no matter how 'good' the site and 'attractive' the building."[1]

The value of a property means the dollar "value" the buyer attaches to the property. The value today stands for the flow of income the buyer anticipates from the property in future years. For example, if the buyer wants a 10% return and says "That apartment building is worth $500,000," the buyer is really saying, "In my opinion, that apartment building is capable of producing income of $50,000 a year for as far ahead as I can see. The value, today, of that annual cash flow of income is a $500,000 by me to get it."

Converting cash flow of a property to a price is relatively easy using this formula:

$$P_0 = NOI / \text{capitalization rate}$$

Known as the Income Capitalization Approach, this approach is most commonly used for investment properties and has as its premises the calculation of "net operating income" capitalized at a rate (the "capitalization rate") commensurate with the risk and life expectancy of the building to find a price (P_0). We discuss how to calculate capitalization rate and NOI below.

1. Capitalization Rate

First, what is meant by the "capitalization rate" (or "cap rate")? The cap rate converts moving cash flows in the future into a specific dollar figure today. The cap rate expresses the informed opinion of the investor; what the investor would currently pay to receive those cash flows from the property for years in the future. The cap rate is expressed as a percentage and is loosely synonymous with initial yield. The example of the $500,000 apartment building (the price, P_0 at current Year 0) above used a 10% cap rate:

$$P_0 = NOI / \text{capitalization rate}$$
$$\$500,000 = \$50,000 / 10\%$$

Remember, an investor is not buying the sticks and bricks, but the cash flow—or more accurately, the investor's financial assumptions about the future cash flow of the building based on property's past performance. The value of the building depends upon the present value of its cash flows. Those interested in the stock market will note the cap rate is the inverse of the price/earnings ratio for stocks. The cap rate is the earnings/price ratio, or NOI/P_0. In the example, the NOI is $50,000. If the current market for such properties required a 10% return, then an all-cash purchase price requires the buyer to come up with $500,000 (50,000/10% = $500,000). In essence, a yearly $50,000 return on the amount invested, $500,000, would be a 10% return.

Another simple financial measurement is the Gross Rent Multiplier (GRM). The GRM can be used to compare properties without regard to operating expenses, NOI, or debt. A property with gross rents of $100,000 and a GRM of 5 would be worth $100,000 x 5, or $500,000.

There are two other classic approaches used in estimating value: (1) the Cost Approach and (2) the Sales (or Market) Comparison Approach. Under the Cost Approach, the investor finds the value of the land and adds this value to the cost to reproduce or replace the building, less any loss of value (depreciation) as the result of physical deterioration and functional obsolescence of the property over time. Under the Sales (or Market) Comparison Approach, the investor compares the property to other properties that have sold in the recent past. Adjustments are then made for differences in time, size, location, condition, and other characteristics between the property under consideration and the comparable properties. The Income Capitalization Approach, discussed above, is normally used for income producing properties over these other two approaches and so is the focus of our discussion.

For those more financially inclined, the cap rate formula is like the equation for the present value of an annuity. An annuity is a regular, periodic flow of payments. To determine today's value (the present value) of regular payments, such as $50,000 per year, we use this:

$$PV \text{ perpetual annuity} = CF / r$$
Or with real estate:
$$P_0 = NOI / \text{cap rate}$$

The value of today's cash flow (PV of a perpetual annuity) is determined by the expected cash flow in the future (CF), divided by a discount rate (r), which is analogous to the value of a property determined by the NOI divided by the capitalization rate. The discount rate (r) may reflect the risk-free rate on government treasuries, e.g., 5%; or the market rate of thirty-year mortgages, e.g., 8%; or riskier investments, e.g., 10% for the property with a cash flow of $50,000 per year in our example.

The cap rate is influenced by the risk of the investment. The greater the risk, the higher the cap rate, and the higher the initial yield the investor expects from the property to compensate the investor for the risk. To illustrate, if the investor thought the property with $50,000 cash flow were even riskier, the investor may use a higher cap rate, say 12%, rather than the 10% used before. This would have the effect of lowering the purchase price for the property:

$$P_0 = NOI / \text{cap rate} = \$50,000 / 12\% = \$416,667.$$

The investor would pay only $416,667, not $500,000, reflecting the investor's expectation of a higher yield as compensation for the risk. By lowering the price for the same cash flow, the investor increases the yield.

Risk for a property is reflected in the cap rate. Four main considerations affect cap rate:

1. *Age*: As a property ages, its useful life, and its ability to generate income, decline. The present value of the remaining cash flow (what the investor is buying) is less now than when the property was first built, or even when the property was purchased by its current owner. For example, when buying an older building, the investor must repair major mechanicals that have reached the end of their useful life. Galvanized piping lasts seventy-five years. A building seventy-five years old may begin to experience severe plumbing problems, increasing the uncertainty of maintenance expenses, which, in turn, affect the certainty of cash flow. With more uncertainty, there is more risk; more risk means a higher cap rate.

2. *Tenant Issues:* Two tenant issues justify an increase in the cap rate. First, the building may experience high vacancy. Vacancy diminishes the certainty of cash flow as a result of tenant rollover, collection expenses, re-leasing and marketing costs. Second, the building may have month-to-month tenants rather than tenants on year-long leases. Month-to-month tenants create uncertainty because tenants are free to move at any time on very short notice. The investor does not know when tenants will move or the amount of rent each unit will generate over the next year. Again, with more risk, the investor should use a higher cap rate.

3. *Neighborhood:* The property's neighborhood also affects the cap rate. It is said that the three things to know about real estate are these: "location, location, location." The cap rate allows the investor to factor location into a property's value. For example, a good property in a strong neighborhood may command a 7% cap rate. A good property in a less desirable neighborhood may justify only a 10% cap rate.

4. *Interest Rates:* On a macroeconomic scale, investors sometimes try to gauge how interest rates affect cap rates. As a rule, when interest rates decrease, making it **less** expensive to borrow money, cap rates also decline, making it **more** expensive to buy property. As interest rates decrease, so do cap rates. The idea is that, as money becomes cheaper (and therefore less risky), sellers think potential buyers can afford to pay more for a property and will accept a lower rate of return—expressed in the cap rate— because there is less risk.

An investor should not take the cap rate so literally that it obscures the robust point that comes out of the discussion above. The cap rate is only a tool. The cap rate adjusts for risk, but is sometimes based on little more than informed guesswork.

As long as the investor is consistent with how that investor utilizes the cap rate, the cap rate may be used to compare different properties. Suppose two properties are within a few blocks of each other, the same age, condition, tenant, and unit mix. If one property generates $50,000 per year, and the other $60,000 per year, the investor would know, using the same cap rate, that there is a $100,000 difference in value:

$$P_0 = \text{NOI} / \text{capitalization rate}$$
$$P_0 \text{ Building 1} = \$50,000/10\% = \$500,000$$
$$P_0 \text{ Building 2} = \$60,000/10\% = \$600,000$$

If Building One had an asking price of $575,000, and Building Two had an asking price of $610,000, the investor's time may be better spent negotiating with the seller of Building Two. The value of Building Two is $600,000, $10,000 within the asking price.

2. Net Operating Income

Once having determined the capitalization rate, the investor now needs to calculate NOI, or net operating income. NOI is the second part of the formula to determine Price, $P_0 = \text{NOI}/\text{cap rate}$. NOI is simply the difference between the annual income collected for the property less the operating expenses.

"Income" includes all revenue generated by the property: rent, laundry, parking, and miscellaneous fees. Rent is, of course, the largest part of income. Typically, the investor will look at past income and project the scheduled income for the next year based on the rent for each unit determined by a rent roll and existing leases on the property. The investor should apply a figure for vacancy and bad debt (sometimes called "physical and economic vacancy"), usually expressed as a percentage of revenue, such as 5%. The vacancy/bad debt allowance is based on the property's ability to attract tenants, the age of the property, tenant issues (unit mix and length of leases, if any), the neighborhood, and the current owner's experience with the building. A strong building may have only a 3% vacancy / bad debt loss, whereas a less attractive building may have 10% vacancy/loss. The difference between the scheduled income and the allowance for vacancy / bad debt is called effective gross income. Operating expenses are then subtracted from effective gross income to arrive at net operating income (see initial proforma below).

Income is pretty straightforward. The calculation of operating expenses, which are subtracted from income, however, is more problematic. For operating expenses, the investor must make assumptions about repairs, maintenance, unit turns, and the overall condition of the property. Nonetheless, an investor may start with the owner's expenses for the building in the last year. The current owner should have records reflecting taxes, utilities (gas, electric, water, sewer), and other operating expenses. Because the owner's information is based on last year's expenses, the investor should *increase* each of the figures to reflect a best estimate of upcoming expenses, perhaps using the rate of inflation in a given year, such as 3%.

Putting all figures together, the investor generates an initial proforma, which might look like this one based on an actual transaction:

APARTMENT COMPLEX
43 UNITS, CHICAGO, ILLINOIS

Gross Income	$228,360
Vac 6%	(13,702)
Bad Debt 1.5%	(3,425)
Other Income	1,000
Effective Gross	212,233
Operating Expenses	
Tax	41,340
Insurance	5,232
Gas	21,000
Electric	2,364
Water/Sewer	4,120
Scavenger	2,700
Maintenance	21,500
Payroll (Janitor)	10,750
Admin & Gen.	1,500
Exterminating	500
Misc.	2,000

Marketing	1,982
Management 5%	10,612
Reserve 5%	10,612
TOTAL	(136,211)
Expected NOI	$76,022

The amounts in the example are not as important as understanding how NOI may be determined using this template. Many of the expenses, like insurance and utilities, are based on hard data from the prior year. On the other hand, some expenses, such as maintenance and reserves, are more subjective, based on the history of repairs, age, and condition of the building, which may be difficult to determine with any precision. For example, in the above proforma, the investor estimated $500 per apartment for maintenance (43 units x $500 = $21,500). As it turned out, real maintenance expenses exceeded $32,000 for the first year, or about $750 per unit. The $10,612 contingency allowance ("reserve" in the proforma) protected the investor from a $10,500 cash call. The "reserve" was nothing more than a plug-number based on 5% of Effective Gross Income and represents the investor's best estimate to cover unknown future costs.

Some investors also budget a replacement reserve to account for replacement of major appliances and capital improvements. In a forty-three-unit building, the investor may expect to replace three refrigerators per year—say, at a cost of $400 each. The proforma would include a replacement reserve for refrigerators of $1,200 per year (3 x $400). The investor may expect the roof will need work in five years at a cost of $10,000. The proforma would include a line item for roof reserve at $2,000 per year ($10,000/5). Reserves differ from other operating expenses in that they are not actually used, but put aside and utilized when needed. Investors may be reluctant to use replacement reserves in the initial proforma because some reserves are high and make no allowance for use of money upon a refinancing of the property. Proceeds from a loan refinance often go toward capital improvements. In addition, replacement reserves are difficult to calculate on the initial proforma and may be better left for subsequent operating budgets as the investor becomes more familiar with the property.

D

Complex Analysis: Growth and Crunching the Numbers (Continued)

The initial proforma and formula (P_0 = NOI / cap rate) provide the investor with a reasonable way to value a property. The problem is this simple formula does not give a property credit for income growth through rent increases, or appreciation in the value of the property that may be realized upon sale. Some investors do not estimate appreciation as part of their return because appreciation depends on too many factors that cannot be controlled. Nevertheless, income growth and appreciation can be factored into the purchase price.

A more complex analysis using the same NOI and cap rate calculations may factor income growth and appreciation into the purchase price. The main value of the more complex analysis over the rough and ready approach used in the initial proforma is that the complex analysis forces the prospective purchaser to think through the entire investment process: acquisition, ownership, and sale, while still giving the purchaser firm yardsticks for comparing different properties. Because the complex analysis looks further into the future, it has some obvious shortcomings. Foremost, it requires assumptions about the future that may be no more than guesses.[2]

43 UNIT APARTMENT BUILDING, CHICAGO

	Year 1	Year 2	Year 3	Year 4	Year 5	Year 6	Year 7
Gross Income	228,360	234,069	239,921	245,919	252,067	258,368	264,828
Vac 6.0%	(13,702)	(14,044)	(14,395)	(14,755)	(15,124)	(15,502)	(15,890)
Bad Debt 1.5%	(3,425)	(3,511)	(3,599)	(3,689)	(3,781)	(3,876)	(3,972)
Other Income	1,000	1,025	1,051	1,077	1,104	1,131	1,160
Effective Gross	212,233	217,539	222,977	228,552	234,266	240,122	246,125
Operating Expenses							
Tax	41,340	42,167	43,010	43,870	44,748	45,643	46,556
Insurance	5,232	5,337	5,443	5,552	5,663	5,777	5,892
Gas	21,000	21,420	21,848	22,285	22,731	23,186	23,649
Electric	2,364	2,411	2,460	2,509	2,559	2,610	2,662
Water/Sewer	4,120	4,120	4,202	4,286	4,372	4,460	4,549
Scavenger	2,700	2,754	2,809	2,865	2,923	2,981	3,041
Maintenance	21,500	21,500	21,930	22,369	22,816	23,272	23,738
Payroll(Janitor)	10,750	10,965	11,184	11,408	11,636	11,869	12,106
Admin & Gen.	1,500	1,545	1,591	1,639	1,688	1,739	1,791
Exterminating	500	515	530	546	563	580	597
Misc.	2,000	2,060	2,122	2,185	2,251	2,319	2,388
Marketing	1,982	2,041	2,082	2,124	2,166	2,210	2,254
Management 5%	10,612	10,877	11,149	11,428	11,743	12,006	12,306
Reserve 5%	10,612	10,877	11,094	11,316	11,543	11,774	10,750
TOTAL	136,211	138,589	141,456	144,384	147,372	150,423	152,279
Expected NOI	76,022	78,950	81,521	84,168	86,893	89,699	93,846
Present Value @14%		66,686	60,749	55,024	49,834	45,130	40,866
DEBT 1ˢᵗ Mortgage	68,184	68,184	68,184	68,184	68,184	68,184	68,184
2ⁿᵈ Mortgage			3,279	3,279	3,279	3,279	3,279
Pension	2,048	2,048	2,048	2,048	2,048	2,048	2,048
CASH FLOW	5,790	8,718	8,010	10,657	13,382	16,188	20,335

PV of Disposition

Expected NOI (Yr 7)	93,846
Capitalization rate	11.50%
Expected sale price	816,053
Less 2%	(16,321)
Net Disposition Funds	799,732
PV sale year 6 @ 14%	364,347

Summary of PV Contributors

Cap Rate	11.5%		1st Mortgage	2d Mortgage	Pension
Year 1	66,686	**Loan**	680,800	36,375	25,000
Year 2	60,749	**Year 1**	(7,678)	(233)	
Year 3	55,024	**Year 2**	(8,393)	(250)	
Year 4	49,834	**Year 3**	(9,174)	(292)	(270)
Year 5	45,130	**Year 4**	(10,028)	(317)	(291)
Year 6	40,866	**Year 5**	(10,961)	(344)	(313)
From disposition	364,347	**Year 6**	(11,982)	(374)	(337)
TOTAL	682,636	**TOTAL**	(58,216)	(1,327)	(1,694)
		Balance	622,584	35,048	23,306

LEVERAGED IRR	0	1	2	3	4	5	6
	(13,500)	5,790	8,718	8,010	10,657	13,382	134,982
IRR	77.92%						

To compare the two approaches, the initial proforma suggested the property would be worth (the investor assumes a 11.5% cap rate):

$$P_0 = \text{NOI} / \text{cap rate} = \$76,022 / 11.5\% = \$661,061$$

Whereas the more detailed analysis suggests a purchase price of $682,636 (see "total" under Summary of PV Contributors).

The difference between the two methods? The initial proforma is like a snapshot, looking only at what the expected NOI will be by the end of the first year of ownership. The more complex analysis, however, is like a moving picture, looking at the property from acquisition year 0, growth in cash flows years 1-6, to the eventual sale of the property, which in this example is assumed to occur at the end of year 6, although the sale could be calculated in any year the investor thought reasonable.

IRR stands for "internal rate of return." IRR is the rate which the sum of the present value of cash flows = 0. IRR is a handy tool to find a rate of return given a set of known cash flows. The more complex analysis assumed a discount rate of 14% (11.5% cap rate and 2.5% growth). IRR assumes the discount rate is *unknown*. In the example, assuming an investment of -$13,500 (the number is negative, reflecting cash out), the property generates a positive stream of cash flow. What is the rate of return on this cash flow? IRR tells us this cash flow is equal to a 77.92% return on the leveraged $13,500 investment. Mathematically, discounting each cash flow for the year it is spent (present) or received (years 1-6), and adding all the cash flows, PV is 0 at a 77.92% rate of return:

Present	Year 1	Year 2	Year 3	Year 4	Year 5	Year 6	
-13,500 +	5,790	+ 8,718	+ 8,010	+ 10,657	+ 13,382	+ 134,982	=0
	$(1+77.92\%)$	$(1+77.92\%)^2$	$(1+77.92\%)^3$	$(1+77.92\%)^4$	$(1+77.92\%)^5$	$(1+77.92\%)^6$	

Discounting of cash flows, and why discounting is important, is discussed immediately below. (By the way, the $134,982 amount in Year 6 is found by taking the Cash Flow in Year 6 of $16,188, adding the sale proceeds after costs of sales—calculated below—of $799,732, less the balance of all the loans on the property, so that we have: $16,188 + $799,732 - $622,584 - $35,048 - $23,306 = $134,982.)

Because the complex analysis calculates cash flows over time, it is necessary to bring all cash flows back to the same point in time—today—so the value of each cash flow can be compared with the others. To compare cash flows received at different times, each cash flow must be discounted to its present value. The concept of present value recognizes the time value of money; a dollar today is worth more than a dollar one year from now. (To illustrate, ask yourself which would you rather have: $100 today or $100 a year from now? At a minimum, with $100 today, you can put the $100 in a bank, earn interest, and have $100 plus interest a year from now.) If the cash flows were not discounted, the analysis would be faulty for not recognizing that each cash flow is received at a different time.

The present value of each cash flow is calculated by this formula:

$$\text{Present Value} = \text{Cash Flow} / (1 + \text{discount rate})^{time}$$

To calculate the present value of a cash flow, two new concepts are introduced: time and the discount rate.

The exponent, time, is the year in which the cash flow is expected (2 for year two, 3 for year three, and so on). For simplicity, the analysis assumes each cash flow is received at the end of the year. The cash flows could be calculated on a monthly basis and discounted to present value for each month, but the additional math would not yield much difference for the purposes of our analysis. Time in $(1 + \text{discount rate})^t$ is the year in which the buyer expects to receive the cash flow.

For example, we will assume the discount rate is the sum of the cap rate (11.5%) and the growth rate in rents (2.5%), or 14%. Putting all the information together, the present value of the cash flow NOI expected at the end of year two (see "NOI" under Year 2) equals:

$$PV = \$78{,}950 / (1.14)^2 = \$60{,}749$$

This tells us that $78,950 is worth, today, $60,749 with a 14% discount rate. The discounting of NOI to present value is done for each of the six years we assume the property is owned. To complete the investment cycle, it is necessary to estimate a sales price. If the investor expects no material change in the condition, tenant quality, or neighborhood, the investor may use the same capitalization rate (11.5%). With the growth in cash flows, by Year 7, the investor anticipates NOI to have grown to $93,846 (see "NOI under Year 7—that is the amount the buyer would expect to get in the upcoming year when the buyer purchases the property at the end of Year 6). Applying the pricing formula, the investor expects to sell the property for:

$$P_6 = \text{NOI} / \text{cap rate} = \$93{,}846 / 11.5\% = \$816{,}053$$

After subtracting an estimated 2% of the sale price for selling costs, the investor will receive net sale proceeds of $799,732. But the investor will not receive the sale proceeds for another six years, so like all other cash flows, the sale proceeds must be discounted to their present value:

$$\text{PV net sale proceeds} = \$799,732 / (1.14)^6 = \$364,347$$

It is only a matter of adding all the expected cash flows for each of the six years of ownership, discounted to their present value, to arrive at a current purchase price:

Year 1	66,686
Year 2	60,749
Year 3	55,024
Year 4	49,834
Year 5	45,130
Year 6	40,866
From disposition	364,347
TOTAL	682,636

The investor is buying the expected cash flows of the property. In this case, the investor has determined, "I will pay up to $682,636 for the right to receive those cash flows." Obviously, the investor would like to pay less than $682,636, but should not pay more. By the way, these calculations were based on an actual transaction where the asking price for this property was $895,000, demonstrating that the asking price should not be used as a guide to determine a property's worth. In this case, the investor would either pass on this property or negotiate a significant reduction in price, as was actually done, to justify purchase.

In summary, the complex analysis considers the *amount* of money to be received each year, *when* that amount will be received (the more distant in time the payment, the less its value), the *length of time* over which the building will be held and finally, the building's *expected value* at the end of the investment period (the building's residual value).

E

Factors Influencing Growth in Cash Flows

In making projections, the investor generally assumes rent and expenses tend to rise while the investor holds the property, and the property can therefore be sold for more than its initial purchase price. Thus, a property's price increases with growth in cash flows. Growth in cash flows comes from two places: (i) inflation and (ii) the ability of the property to pass through inflation in the form of higher rents.

Growth can be thought of as the product of the inflation rate and the property's ability to pass through inflation to the tenants in the form of higher rents:

$$G = i\lambda$$

where: G = growth

i = inflation, expressed in percent

λ = pass-through rate, expressed in percent

The complex analysis assumed a 100% pass-through rate (2.5% x 100% = 2.5%). A 100% pass-through rate, however, may not be realistic if the property is in poor condition, in a declining neighborhood, or in an area of high vacancy rates. In any of these cases, the inflation pass-through rate may be less than 100%. Over time, a lower pass-through rate, such as 50%, will mean growth at only half the rate of inflation (2.5% x 50% = 1.25%). A lower pass-through rate will erode cash flows, and ultimately, the price the property may command upon resale.

Generally, apartment buildings enjoy higher pass-through rates because of the length of residential tenancies. Each time a lease is renewed or unit re-rented, the property owner has an opportunity to increase rents. Residential leases have a shorter duration than most other property types:

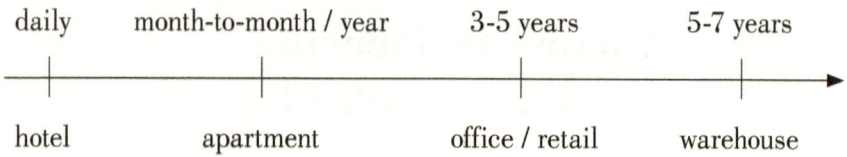

In apartment buildings, space is re-rented to new tenants or leases are renewed with existing tenants at least annually. The apartment market is characterized by shorter, standardized leases and less tenant sophistication (and therefore more market power by the property owner). No one tenant is large enough to demand special concessions. In times of inflation, the property owner does not have to wait to pass through rent increases. The property owner may increase a tenant's rent upon lease renewal, and if the tenant does not agree, the tenant has to leave. Loss of one tenant in a sixty-unit building will make little difference on the property's cash flow. Apartment rollover will capture significant inflation hedging qualities the investor expects from real estate.

The omnipresent hand of government is proof of the market power of apartment owners. Consumer protection laws are becoming increasing popular as a check on the owners' market power. For example, the Chicago Landlord Tenant Ordinance imposes strict liability on apartment owners for a variety of economic pecadillos, such as awarding a tenant double the security deposit for the owner's failure to pay interest on a tenant's deposit. In such cases, owners face a large liability over a small interest payment. In the case of *Lawrence v. Regent Realty*, the Illinois Supreme Court has said the Chicago law is "unbalanced" and "totally disproportionate" to any potential loss suffered, but nonetheless, felt constrained to affirm an award of large statutory penalties to a tenant over a small pet deposit. It is not unusual that tenant protection laws fail to have any safe-harbor provisions for owners who unknowingly and unintentionally violate them.

F

Qualitative Factors Influencing Price

Net operating income, cap rate, and growth in cash flows are not the only influences on value. Qualitative factors also affect value. Each piece of property is unique; each property has a different curb appeal. In residential real estate, where tenant decisions are often more emotional than financial ("Would I want to live here?"), the real estate investor must measure the intangible aspects of the property that will affect the property's ability to attract tenants. The guide below attempts to quantify the various intangible and emotive characteristics of a property:[3]

QUALITATIVE RATING GUIDE
FOR RESIDENTIAL REAL ESTATE

I. NEIGHBORHOOD
  1. Strong and stable — 10
  2. Good — 8
  3. Fair and static — 6
  4. Fair but declining — 4
  5. Poor and static — 2
  6. Poor and declining — 0

   - Transition to improving neighborhood (add) — +1

II. PARKING AND TRANSIT

1.	Excellent off-street parking and good public transit	10
2.	Limited off-street parking and good public transit	8
3.	Limited off-street parking and fair public transit	6
4.	Limited on-street parking only and good to fair public transit	4
5.	No parking and fair transit	2
6.	No parking and poor or no public transit	0

III. RECREATION AND PARKS

1.	Near park, beach, or recreation	10
2.	Not near park, beach, or recreation	0

IV. PHYSICAL CONDITION AND APPEARANCE

1.	Excellent	10
2.	Very Good—little deferred maintenance and curable obsolescence	8
3.	Good—some deferred maintenance and curable obsolescence	6
4.	Fair—much deferred maintenance and curable obsolescence	4
5.	Poor—much deferred maintenance and curable/incurable obsolescence	2
6.	Very poor condition and appearance	0

V. TENANT STABILITY

A. Leases
  1. All units — 3
  2. Some units — 2
  3. Month-to-month — 1

B. Credit
  1. Good — 3
  2. Moderate — 2
  3. Poor or unknown — 1

C. Security Deposits
  1. Greater than one month — 3
  2. Equal to one month — 2
  3. Less than one month, or some units — 1
  Unstable and undesirable — 0

VI. AVAILABLE FINANCING

1. Seller financing — 10
2. Some (> 10%) seller take back, at/or below market — 8
3. Some (< 10%) seller take back — 6
4. No seller financing — 0

RATING

AAA	55-59
AA	45-54
A	35-44
B	25-34
C	15-24
D	<15

A value is assigned for each of the six sections. From each section, the property's score is totaled. The intangible characteristics of a property are rated from a triple A to D grade investment. The guide may measure physical characteristics of the building—its design, attractiveness—or the neighborhood. For example, physical deterioration is evidenced by wear and tear, decay, dry rot, cracks, and structural defects in the building. Physical deterioration is normally considered curable. Short-lived items suffer from faster deterioration. Inherent depreciation to long-lived items may remain because it is often not economically feasible, nor necessary, to repair these items. Functional obsolescence occurs when there are defects in design, or circumstances have changed over time so some aspects of the structure, floor plan, or overall layout of the apartment is obsolete. External obsolescence results from unfavorable externalities that affect the property, such as high vacancies or low rent levels that will not support new construction, lack of available financing, or interest in the neighborhood. Generally speaking, external obsolescence is incurable.

Each investor may develop their own rating scale to judge characteristics important to their ownership decision. In determining what a property is worth, the qualitative rating should corroborate the quantitative factors found in the cap rate, net operating income and growth in cash flows for the particular property under consideration.

End Notes

1. J. Graaskamp, *Graaskamp on Real Estate*, Urban Land Institute, (Stephen Jarchow editor, 1991), pp. 376-77.
2. The complex analysis and discussion about growth in cash flows are based on J. Webb and J. Pagliari, Jr., "The Characteristics of Real Estate Returns and Their Estimation," in *The Handbook of Real Estate Portfolio Management*, (Pagliari, editor, 1995), pp. 177-184.
3. Based on A. Arnold and I. Kusnet, "Analyzing a Real Estate Investment," *Real Estate Review Portfolio* No. 4, (1981), pp. F1-F5.

III

NEGOTIATION: CLOSING THE DEAL

Someone once complained that their first adventure negotiating convinced them the whole process was as unstable as a one-wheeled rickshaw on a downhill course, with the steering control manned alternatively by one side, then by the other side, each side intent upon veering the contraption in opposite directions of the road. A definition for negotiations is not far from this description: Negotiations are the act of back and forth communication to reach an agreement.

Having witnessed several hundred negotiations firsthand, there are certain principles that, when conscientiously applied, will lead to better negotiations. These principals are tools that establish a framework for thinking about negotiations, introduce prescriptive suggestions for improving decisions to reduce the likelihood of impasse, and make it easier to reach an agreement by expanding the benefits both parties receive.

Virtually all real estate negotiations occur in a two party context: a seller on one side, and a buyer on the other. Buyers and sellers complete a symbiotic relationship between those wishing to buy property and those wishing to sell, thereby keeping the market active. There may be other constituents, such as lenders, brokers, tenants, or local government officials—all who may have preferences that need to be taken into account. At the formative stage of the deal, however, the preferences of the seller and buyer will dominate negotiations.

Before beginning any important negotiation, the investor should consider three core issues:

1. Who are the seller and buyer
2. What are the buyer's preferences
3. What are the seller's preferences

Each of these issues is discussed below. In section A, we review buyer and seller personalities, and how personalities affect real estate negotiations. Next, in section B, we analyze buyer and seller preferences, letters of intent, intermediaries, the "3 Ps" of negotiating, "active listening" to get information, and the use of a decision tree to anticipate seller terms. Finally, in section C, we discuss integrative negotiations, which increase the likelihood of reaching an agreement.

A

Seller and Buyer Personalities

The first core issue, who the seller and buyer are, is not an inquiry about biographical information. Biographical information may be useful; and some biographical data, such as age and prior experience, should be known about the parties to the negotiation. An older seller may be tired of the management headaches and just looking to get out of the property. This seller may be willing to finance the purchase of the property by holding paper (a note and a mortgage) if the payments are reasonably certain. On the other hand, a younger seller may want to trade up into a larger property and may want as much cash as possible, so seller financing will be out of the question. For our purposes, who the seller and buyer are asks a more fundamental question: what are the seller's and buyer's personalities?[1]

By knowing something about the seller and buyer personalities, the buyer may adapt negotiations to the personality styles involved. After defining the seller's personality, the buyer can place what the seller says and how the seller responds in a context that will provide more meaningful negotiations.

There are four personality styles in real estate negotiations:

Personality Table

		EMOTIONALISM	
		HIGH	LOW
ASSERTIVENESS	HIGH	Extrovert	Pragmatic
	LOW	Amiable	Analytical

Each personality style negotiates differently. If one personality style has a common characteristic with another (pragmatic and analytical both have low emotionalism, or the pragmatic and the extrovert are both highly assertive), the more compatible the negotiators will be with each other. Conversely, if there is not a common characteristic, there will be less compatibility. The pragmatic and amiable personalities are at opposite ends of the emotive and assertiveness spectrums and, therefore, are opposite each other in the personality matrix. People may be a combination of two or three styles, but one style will probably dominate.

Although the personality styles may be recognized along two characteristics, assertiveness and emotionalism, there are several defining traits that will affect how a buyer should deal with each personality:

- *Pragmatic.* Bottom line oriented, assertive, fact focused, take-charge personality. A pragmatic is concerned about time management and will be good about responding to an offer promptly. A pragmatic makes decisions quickly and will expect the other side to do so as well. This personality type wants answers in response to questions, avoids small talk, and anticipates if the other side leaves a phone mail message, the message will be time efficient, containing terms and content of an offer so the pragmatic may make a meaningful response, not simply "call me."

- *Extrovert.* People oriented, enthusiastic, emotional, assertive personality. An extrovert loves to be around people, is not punctual, and will expect small talk about vacation, family, or friends. Although assertive like the pragmatic, the extrovert is not necessarily efficient. An extrovert dislikes detail, has a short attention span, and skips around to different issues, and so has to make decisions quickly. Though a quick decision maker, an extrovert will expect time for lunch meetings, socializing, and face-to-face negotiations.
- *Amiable.* People oriented, emotional, laid-back personality. An amiable wants to be surrounded by people with similar interests and enjoys talking about people and their interests to develop trust. An amiable has no need to be in control and sets up barriers to avoid high-pressure situations. Wanting to be liked, an amiable cannot say no, needs time to think over decisions, and dislikes change. An amiable wants face-to-face negotiations and is suspicious of fast decision makers who may appear cold or hardheaded (like the pragmatic).
- *Analytical.* Detail oriented, fact focused, nonassertive personality. An analytical likes lots of information and investigation, is cautious about decision-making, and is nonconfrontational. This personality type wants accurate information in response to questions, charts and graphs and time for more investigation. An analytical does not appear to need control but may in fact have it by delaying decisions. Never shooting from the hip, an analytical perceives quick decision makers as too flippant or error prone.

From the four personality styles, there are different ways to make and respond to an offer on a real estate transaction. A pragmatic will not mind a phone call to discuss important terms and will pride himself on being a quick decision maker. Being "decisive" is a compliment, so long as the pragmatic feels they have control over the negotiations. An extrovert would consider a phone call impersonal and would rather meet over lunch to discuss an offer. Before getting down to business, however, the extrovert would want to hear about a recent vacation or upcoming sporting event. An extrovert makes quick decisions but will mix business with pleasure. An amiable would like a lunch meeting to discuss terms, if the parties have spoken before, either over the phone or through their brokers so the amiable knows something about the background, family, and interests of the other side. The amiable will be concerned how the other side feels about an offer and will be put off if they believe they are forced to make a major decision on the spot. Finally, the analytical wants offers and counteroffers in writing to be able to analyze terms and crunch numbers. An analytical would not mind a lunch meeting if papers were brought to the table and the parties were able to exchange further information.

Personalities may include national background, which will add a layer of complexity to the negotiations. The United States follows an egalitarian, informal approach to negotiations. Titles are not particularly important. Use of first names quickly in negotiations minimizes status differences and promotes equality and informality. Other countries, however, are more hierarchical and formal than the United States. The Japanese, for example, like to know a person's title within their company to know how to address them. In Germany, negotiators would never address someone by their first name, especially not a negotiator on the other side of the table. In Spain and Central and South America, the *usted* form of address (formal "you") is used. A first-name address would severely insult the sense of propriety and formality. Consequently, knowing information about the "who" is essential to any successful negotiation.

In summary, the personality styles may be placed along a spectrum:

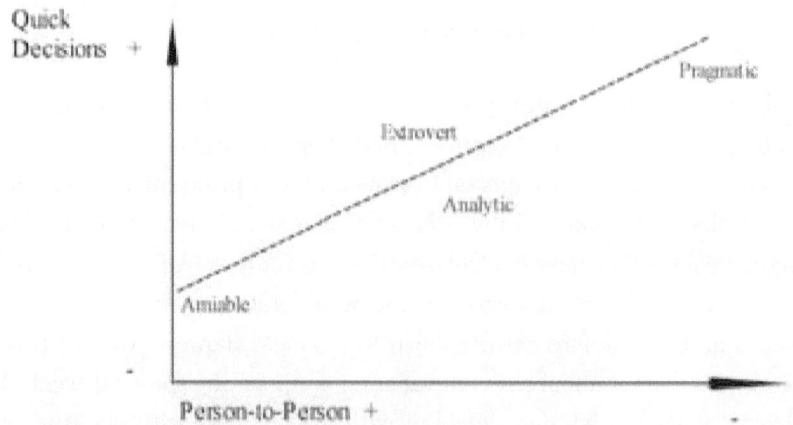

The personality table provides a couple of benefits. First, it allows the buyer to reduce a world of enormous cognitive complexity into terms of four general personality types, thereby making it easier to code the personalities and, to some extent, the actions of the people around the buyer. Second, by understanding the personalities involved, the buyer is far more likely to communicate well with others. Knowing his or her own personality, and that of the seller, the buyer will be able to get the seller off demands the seller may have imposed on the negotiations because of personality style and focus on preferences. The buyer will be able to gauge how to make an offer, how to effectively respond to a counteroffer, and how to avoid turning the seller off because the seller thinks the buyer is rude, uncooperative, or just plain unfriendly.

B

Seller and Buyer Preferences

After identifying the personalities to the negotiation, the buyer wants to understand their own preferences—what is important? The term *preference* is more descriptive of the negotiating process than *position*. Position connotes a steadfast point, anchored without regard to terms around it; whereas a preference suggests a tendency for change, a codependency of one term on another, and more closely defines the ebb and flow reality of negotiation.

The numbers help define preferences: purchase price (how much will the buyer pay), financing (how much is needed and at what cost), and cash flow. Preferences guide the buyer to a bottom line. If no agreement is reached, preferences collectively serve as a reservation point—a point at which the buyer is indifferent between the deal and an impasse (walking away). The buyer has to be willing to walk away. The seller can easily manipulate the buyer if the buyer "just has to have the property." Instead, the buyer needs to focus on articulating, knowing, and analyzing the buyer's own preference structure.

1. Documents and People as Intermediaries

What often separates a good negotiator from a poor one is a strategic sense, the ability to devise an overall plan, to link moves and initiatives in a way that serves a clear goal. A letter of intent helps the buyer recognize preferences and get feedback from the seller about the seller's own preferences without committing the buyer to purchase the property. A letter of intent is just that—an expression of intent. A letter of intent is different than a contract because the letter of intent allows the buyer to discuss terms without being legally bound to perform.

The letter of intent directs initial negotiations to three or four main issues: price, seller financing (e.g., the seller loans part of the purchase price), and miscellaneous terms, such as buyer credits or commissions, to facilitate further discussions.

Through the letter of intent, the parties have relationship-specific terms. The seller is psychologically less likely to consider an alternative negotiating partner after having invested time to negotiate with this buyer. Once a relationship develops, competitive offers from the outside are less of a threat to the buyer.

Although letters of intent may take many forms, the following is a sample of the terms one such letter of intent may contain:

LETTER OF INTENT

The buyer's lawyers in Chicago will draft a purchase offer and deliver it to the seller within seven (7) days from the date of seller's acceptance of this letter of intent. The buyer is also prepared to place $_____ deposit with its offer. The buyer is willing to enter into negotiations concerning the purchase of (address) on the following terms:

1. *Property.* The property that is the subject of this letter is the place commonly known as (address, city, state) (the "property"), the land, building, improvements, and personal property owned by seller and located on and used in connection with the operation of the property.
2. *Purchase price.* The purchase price for the property will be $_____ The balance of the purchase price not paid described below will be paid in cash by buyer at closing, plus or minus prorations.
3. *Bank financing.* Buyer will secure a loan in the amount of 55% of the purchase price, with interest not to exceed 9% per annum, 1.5 points, 25-year amortization, paid to the seller at

closing. [These terms are for the buyer's benefit so the buyer is not required to accept a loan at higher rates.]

4. *Seller financing.* Buyer and the seller will enter into an agreement under which 35% of the purchase price [so in this example, the buyer anticipates 100%-55%-35%, leaving 10% of the purchase price to be paid in cash] will be in the form of a loan by seller secured by a promissory note payable to seller (the "note"), which will pay interest only, beginning immediately upon closing for a period of ten years at which time the note shall be fully due and payable. The blended interest rate paid over the life of the note will be 7% per annum. The note will be personally guaranteed by the principals of buyer. The note may be sold or assigned by the seller at any time, and may be paid before maturity or upon sale or refinancing of the property without penalty.

5. *Commission.* The parties recognize that the buyer's principal is a licensed broker and, as such, is entitled to a cooperating commission under the listing agreement between seller and listing broker in the amount of 2.5% of the purchase price, which commission may be applied as a credit at closing.

This letter does not constitute a binding offer to purchase and will not, upon execution by the parties, become a binding contract to purchase the property. It is understood that no binding agreement or contract will be created unless and until a real estate sale contract is executed by both parties. Notwithstanding the foregoing, seller agrees not to solicit or accept any formal or informal offers to purchase the property until both parties have revoked this letter.

Very truly yours

/s/ Buyer

ACKNOWLEDGED:

_____
Seller (date)

_____
Print name

Making Money Going into the Deal | 71

The letter of intent discusses price, financing, and one or two other terms, such as buyer credits for a commission. The letter may also include certain other terms, such as any one or more of the following:

- Payments to the seller will be made quarterly, instead of monthly
- Interest may be deferred for the first two years, for example 1.25% will be deferred, to accumulate but not compound
- Seller will accept a "standstill" mortgage, also known as an interest-only mortgage, which provides the buyer with lower payment but no loan amortization
- Seller financing will consist of a "sliding mortgage" starting small, with payments increasing as the cash flow on the property increases
- Seller financing will have a moratorium on payments (e.g., payments to seller will begin twelve months after closing)
- Seller financing will be amortized over forty years instead of the more conventional twenty-five or thirty years
- Seller agrees to subordinate seller financing to any new financing buyer places on property
- Seller will consent to substitution of collateral
- Seller will allow the buyer to "walk the mortgage" from one piece of collateral to another of equal or greater value (thus releasing the first piece of collateral for another use by buyer)
- In lieu of all cash, the seller will accept some cash and barter services—to illustrate, free rent for a unit in the building for a period of years, or a time-share in Hilton Head, South Carolina.
- Instead of fixed payments, seller will accept a 20% participation in the cash flow of the property after debt service (cash flow participation) or a percentage of the net sale proceeds (sale price less costs of sale) from the value of the property when the property is sold (residual participation)
- Seller will guarantee vacancy will not exceed 5% of gross scheduled rents for the first six months, and any amount over a 5% vacancy will be applied as a buyer credit to the amount owed to the seller under the seller financing.

There are many possibilities. All of these terms have been used in transactions at one time or another. (In fact, on one deal, the moratorium on payments to the seller was actually two years without interest!) The buyer trades nonessential terms, like a forty-year amortization schedule or quarterly payments, for concessions more critical to the transaction, such as price or interest rate. The buyer may say to the seller, "If you want a twenty-five-year amortization with monthly payments, you will have to lower the price by $10,000 to fit my underwriting requirements for your property, otherwise the deal won't work." On one transaction, the seller wanted a higher price and was willing to go from a four-month moratorium on payments on seller financing to fifteen months without interest to get a higher price. As grandma used to say, "If you don't ask, you won't get it." So it is usually better to specifically request a term than to wrongly assume the seller will not agree to it and, therefore, not ask.

The letter of intent is an intermediary vehicle, offering the buyer the ability to negotiate without obligating the buyer to purchase the property. A documentary intermediary is one way to create a basis for discussions.

People may also act as intermediaries—a broker, lawyer, or one of the partners in a partnership. Use of an intermediary creates possibilities for discussions by using asymmetric power that allows the buyer to discuss potential contract provisions without binding the buyer to specific terms.

Intermediaries bring detachment to the negotiation process for the buyer:

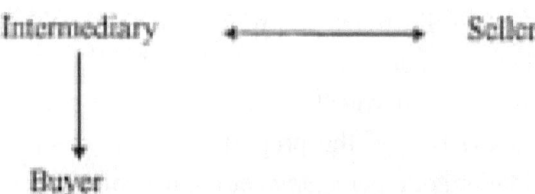

Intermediaries provide face saving and protection from information loss because it is not clear to what extent the intermediary represents actual terms from the buyer. Paradoxically, the buyer strengthens its bargaining abilities as it weakens apparent control over the terms of the negotiation. An intermediary may test a preference, hear the seller's response, then plead lack of authority to commit to any specific terms. Lawyers frequently discuss terms of a settlement with the other side and conclude on a "willing to recommend basis," meaning the lawyer will recommend the terms of the settlement, but the client (who was not present during negotiations) is free to reject it.

Use of intermediaries works both ways, and the buyer has to be cautious. One seller was particularly effective with the use of intermediaries. In this case, the broker contacted the buyer with a "few changes" to the contract. After mentioning each change, the broker would ask for agreement. Point by point, the broker went through the contract with the buyer, obtaining commitment or an opinion from the buyer as to what the buyer may be willing to accept. When finished, the broker professed he lacked authority to agree to any terms but would speak to the seller. Later, the seller's attorney called the buyer. Following a similar exercise, point by point, covering some new points and some of the same points, with still additional concessions from the buyer, the seller's attorney concluded by saying that while the parties seemed to be in agreement, he would have to speak to the seller. The attorney called back the next day, apologizing profusely; the seller rejected several terms on which the buyer thought he had agreement with the seller's intermediaries, and consequently, the buyer had shown a willingness to grant concessions without any reciprocal commitment from the seller.

What was really happening was one-way negotiating. Negotiations occurred without specific commitment from the seller. The buyer fell into several traps.

1. The buyer agreed to negotiate through an intermediary for the seller rather than insisting on equal footing with someone who had authority to make binding decisions. Both the seller's broker and the seller's attorney had to appeal to "higher authority," the seller, who was not present when decisions had to be made during negotiations. The seller learned about the buyer's preferences without the buyer learning about those of the seller. The seller also gained valuable time to review and learn about terms the buyer was willing to accept through the use of intermediaries before making any decision.

2. The buyer began negotiating without knowing the agenda. Worse, the buyer was double-teamed by the seller's broker and the seller's attorney. The buyer should have insisted on suggested changes in writing beforehand to know the scope of the intended modifications to the contract. The buyer should not have begun discussions until the agenda was clear.

3. The buyer allowed the seller to role-play with the intermediaries. The attorney played the good cop, and the seller acted as the bad cop, accepting some changes and rejecting others.

2. The 3 Ps of Negotiating: Preferences, Priorities, and Preparation

To negotiate, the buyer must know his or her own preferences. Preferences serve as a guide—for example, the buyer may have wanted to purchase the property at a certain price but is willing to increase the price if the seller carries back a loan at a lower interest rate. Preferences place the terms of the offer in context and allow the buyer to hear the counteroffer, go back, and rethink the seller's response in light of the buyer's own preferences.

Obviously, the *purpose* of the negotiation is to have the seller and buyer reach an agreement and close the deal. But this purpose—to reach an agreement—is too simple to be of any practical use and ultimately, only the natural and probable consequent of a well-executed negotiation. The purpose of the negotiation has to be broken down into more meaningful components to become steps for implementation.

Before beginning the negotiation, the buyer must know what is important and what is not—the buyer must practice the "3 Ps" of negotiating:

- *Preferences* should be identified
- *Prioritized* and
- *Prepared*

Without knowing the buyer's own preference structure, what is important, and in what order, the buyer will make suboptimal choices.

First, to "identify preferences" means to make a checklist of terms that are important without worrying about rank order. List preferences on one page of paper. If the buyer was told there was no limit, what would the buyer want? The buyer should remember the rule "If you don't ask for it, you won't get it."

Second, to "prioritize preferences" means to rank preferences in order of importance, from those terms with little room to negotiate to those terms that may be conceded quickly. The buyer should put a number next to each preference; 1 being the most important, and higher numbers, 10, 11, etc., being less important. Where there are several preferences of equal ranking, the buyer may designate each within a subset, such as 1A, 1B, etc.

To prioritize preferences does not mean negotiations should occur in a particular order. Average negotiators use sequence planning, discussing preference number 1, then preference number 2, and so on. Skilled negotiations, by contrast, discuss each preference so they appear random. There is no predetermined sequence or order of preferences that would give away the buyer's preference structure.

Third, to "prepare" means to internalize terms, know the terms well enough to avoid becoming discombobulated during negotiations. In practice sessions, the buyer should Recognize, Relate, Assimilate, and Actionize terms, signifying in shorthand $R^2 A^2$ (R-two, A-two); the buyer should mentally review preferences and think about the seller's response. More specifically, $R^2 A^2$ means the buyer should: (1) Recognize by understanding what the seller is saying, (2) Relate by showing the seller that the buyer understands (for example, by simply saying to the seller, "I see"), (3) Assimilate by digesting the seller's statements and thinking about different moves, then (4) Actionize by responding to the seller.

Once the buyer has identified, prioritized, and prepared, how does the buyer know the seller's preferences? The buyer should *listen* to what the seller has to say.

Negotiations are subject to asymmetric information whenever one of the parties involved in a transaction possesses information relevant to the transaction the other party does not have (for example, how much the buyer is really willing to pay, or how little the seller is actually willing to accept). Information can be power in a negotiation. If one side knows something about the other, that side may have better control over the negotiation.

Listening, acknowledging, and encouraging the seller to speak is one way to get information. And the seller will give information because listening is, by nature, nonthreatening. If the buyer must speak, repeat what the seller has said. This technique, like rewinding the tape, is psychologically reassuring to the seller because the buyer appears to understand what the seller has said. At the same time, the buyer is not giving any information away.

When the seller takes a position, the seller will probably have some rationale for that position. The buyer who listens will have a better chance of learning the seller's rationale, what is important to the seller, and why. Human experience yields countless situations in which a group of facts—if believed to exist—can, by inferential reasoning, lead to a related factual conclusion. Although an underlying fact may never be disclosed by the seller, a number and variety of basic facts can lead to an inferential conclusion. Digging into these underlying facts will reveal an array of interests; the preference in dispute may have a different meaning to each of the two parties, making agreement easier to reach once the underlying interests are known.

To get information, the buyer should practice "active listening." Three techniques facilitate active listening: (1) metadiscourse, (2) avoiding disruptors, and (3) silence.

Metadiscourse is a technique by which the buyer describes what the buyer plans to say before saying it—offering a summary, a suggestion, or feelings commentary. "Let me see if I understand your point" or "May I make a suggestion?" or "I'm not sure how to respond, can you help me resolve this?" are all examples of metadiscourse. Metadiscourse allows the buyer to appear to participate in the negotiation without giving any information away. A skilled buyer clarifies its understanding of the seller's offer and attempts to get more information *before* responding. A poor negotiator simply counteroffers.

The second technique, avoiding disrupters, means the buyer should steer clear of words that cause annoyance or make the seller defensive, such as characterizing the buyer's own offer as a "fair price" or on "reasonable terms." Poor negotiators use adjectives that characterize or label positions, which only serve to irritate the other party and disrupt negotiations.

Silence is the third technique. The buyer may encourage the seller with silent signals, a tilted head, raised eyebrows, or a perplexed look. The seller will be tempted to fill the silence with words. Uncomfortable with silence, the seller may assume the negotiations are incomplete and will explain, offering more information. Sometimes silence is wrongly interpreted by the seller as a rejection of the seller's terms, and the seller will respond by making a concession (e.g. reducing the price), or providing more information, before the buyer has said anything.

Using the three techniques of active listening, the buyer has a better chance of knowing the preferences and priorities of the seller. The more accurate the buyer's information is about the seller's preferences and priorities, the more effective the negotiation.

3. Seller Preferences: Decision Tree

After getting information from the seller, the buyer should think about the seller's possible reactions to important terms of an offer. Consider negotiations on price. One of the most important seller preferences will be the price. Suppose a property has a list price of $475,000, and the buyer has offered $440,000. At the most basic level, two things may happen, but obviously only one actually will: the seller will either negotiate with the buyer, or the seller will not.

Based on information from the seller, assume the buyer believes there is a 10% chance the seller will not negotiate and a 90% chance the seller will. Assume further the buyer is willing to pay $450,000 and believes that if the seller will negotiate, the negotiations will be more difficult the further the seller counters from the buyer's $450,000 price, meaning the seller will stick close to its asking price. Negotiations will be difficult (defined by the buyer as a counteroffer by the seller between $465,000 to the list price of $475,000), moderately difficult (between $455,000 and $465,000), and easy (less than $455,000). Again, based on information from the seller, the buyer assigns the likelihood that difficult negotiations will occur at 40%, moderately difficult negotiations at 50%, and easy negotiations at 10%.

A decision tree provides a graphical representation of the decision-making process. A decision tree analyzes decisions when the buyer has no knowledge about which state of nature will occur, when future events are not under the buyer's control. The buyer assigns a probability to each event. Each outcome is a separate branch of the tree. Under this scenario, the buyer's decision tree would look like this:

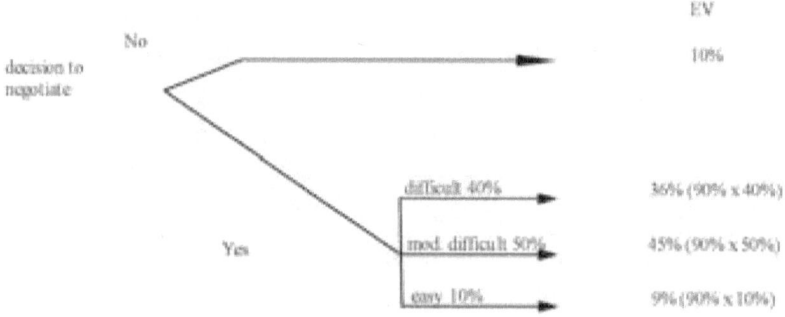

Moving from the left to the right on the decision tree, the tree shows one logical order for the decision-making process. With each branch of the tree, the buyer obtains probability estimates for each possible outcome. The expected value (EV) identifies the most likely outcome, a 45% probability—the seller will negotiate, and at a moderately difficult level.

Why bother with all these machinations? What does the buyer gain from assessing the likelihood of each outcome separately? By separating each outcome, the buyer is able to concentrate on devising a strategy to address the seller's response to the important terms of the buyer's offer. The problem with a simple intuitive approach, or, stated less artfully, flying by the seat of the pants approach, is that the buyer will have to think about more than one thing at a time. While thinking about outcomes, the buyer will also have to be thinking about probabilities, and then combine them. Separating the outcomes and probabilities forces the buyer to give appropriate consideration to the seller's possible counteroffer and the likelihood of each occurring before reaching a decision. The decision tree is a graphical device that sets out a sequence of decisions with several possible outcomes, assigns a probability, and calculates the expected value to focus negotiations on the seller's most likely terms.

C

Integrative Negotiations

The buyer listens, makes an offer. The seller counteroffers, and the buyer listens some more. Negotiations, however, are not always so smooth. Negotiations may become difficult, following a progression of cooperation, problem solving, escalation of controversy, stalemate (both sides refuse to budge), and a return to problem solving and cooperation.[2]

This is the cycle of negotiation:

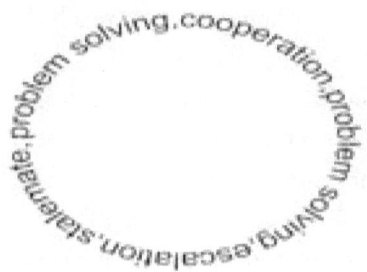

The cycle applies to most negotiations, but now and then, a negotiation may become aberrant and skip or repeat stages in the cycle. For one property, the negotiation became a cha-cha dance, going from "problem solving/stalemate, problem solving/stalemate" for almost a year before the contract was signed.

To minimize stalemate, the parties should negotiate multiple preferences simultaneously. The buyer should not limit negotiations to one issue. To illustrate, in real estate, both sides usually discuss prices early in their negotiations. One-issue negotiations, such as those over price, are inherently distributive. Sellers think about how much they have to gain by selling; whereas buyers view how much they have to give up. In general, the buyer makes an offer that is usually lower than what the buyer will ultimately go, and the seller makes a counteroffer that is usually higher than what the seller expects to end up with. Strictly distributive negotiations occur when two parties bargain along a narrow dimension in search for a middle ground:

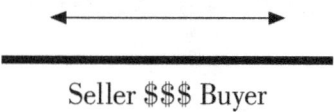

Seller $$$ Buyer

Parties treat negotiations as a fixed pie. What one party gains, the other side must necessarily lose. In a win-lose competition, the seller and buyer assume their interests directly conflict with each other. Skilled negotiators, however, consider negotiations as a smorgasbord, with twice as wide a range of preferences and outcomes as do less skilled negotiators. The greater the number of preferences, the greater the chances for success because there are more items on which to reach an agreement, and ways to avoid purely distributive negotiations.

The parties also make the mistake of handling preferences separately. By treating each preference as separate and distinct, the parties do not have the ability to make trade-offs (such as a higher purchase price in exchange for more favorable seller financing).

As an example, the letter of intent can be used to discuss a trade-off of preferences. Discussing more than just the price, the letter of intent handles multiple preferences contemporaneously and gives the parties more to negotiate with. Integrative negotiations focus on several preferences along a utility line:

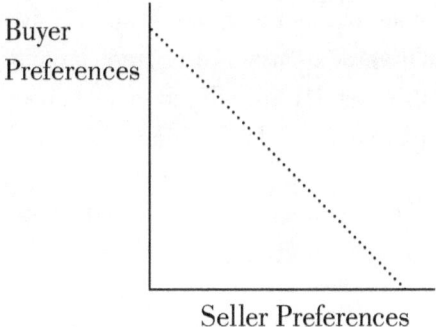

Integrative negotiations are multipreference negotiations. These negotiations can be more productive because they recognize there are a number of preferences available for trade-offs, and the parties have an inherent need for reciprocity. The buyer cannot "command" the seller to accept the buyer's offer. Unlike a court, the buyer cannot order the seller to perform in a certain way or accept a certain price. Consequently, in negotiations, one party gives something to get something.

One way to influence the seller without formal authority is through the rule of reciprocity, the widely held belief that people should be paid back if they do something for someone else. The other party will give only so far before demanding something in return. People tend to reciprocate kindness with kindness, cooperation with cooperation, or hostility with hostility. A cooperative act, or a reputation for being a cooperative person, will likely be reciprocated with cooperation. People will have a tendency to cooperate, until experience shows those with whom they are dealing are taking advantage of them. By acknowledging that there is more than one matter of importance to the seller and making trade-offs, the buyer naturally addresses the seller's need for reciprocity. An integrative negotiation reconciles (i.e., it integrates) through trade-offs to find solutions.

The seller is always listening to the radio station WDIG (What Do I Get?). To resolve the negotiation means the buyer's offer and the seller's counteroffer must converge to a single outcome if there is to be agreement. Every offer ties the buyer's hands to some extent. It says, "This is what I'm willing to do." The offer may expire or be withdrawn later, but while open, the offer carries persuasive power. No longer just an idea or possibility, it is operational and carries the power of positive commitment. The offer itself has the power of invitation, as the buyer says, "I'll agree to that [seller's preferences], if you'll agree to mine," and creates reciprocal behavior.

To summarize this Part III, in order to induce concessionary behavior in the seller, the buyer needs to do the following:

1. Recognize the personalities involved in the negotiation: pragmatic, extrovert, amiable, analytical

2. Secure commitment by stages, using intermediaries or the letter of intent to manifest agreement without being bound

3. Follow the 3 Ps of negotiation by identifying Preferences, Prioritizing preferences, Preparing for the negotiation, *then listen*, using the techniques of active listening, metadiscourse, avoiding disruptors, and employing the judicial use of silence

4. Consider the seller's preferences, perhaps with the use of a decision tree

5. Discuss multiple preferences simultaneously, never separately, to encourage trade-offs.

End Notes

1. The discussion concerning personalities is based in part on Roger Dawson, *The Secrets of Power Negotiating*, cassette tapes (1987).
2. Negotiations follow a picture-frame progression of events, based on D. Pruitt and J. Rubin, *Social Conflict: Escalation, Stalemate, and Settlement* (1986), p. 139.

D

Disorder in the Court

Where one side to a lawsuit cannot get the upper hand, bullying tactics come into play. Lawsuits are an example of the value re-distributing effects that arise when one party cannot gain an upper hand in business. The following is an excerpt from a deposition in an actual case.

First, let us provide a definition of a deposition. (See Stilp, T., "A Model Letter to Witnesses," 82 Ill. Bar Journal 441). A deposition is a question-and-answer session between the attorneys to a lawsuit and a witness. Fundamentally, lawyers take depositions to discover what a witness knows and to preserve testimony for trial. The deposition is usually held in a lawyer's office. Those present are (1) the witness, (2) the court reporter to record the testimony, (3) lawyers for all parties to the lawsuit, and (4) the parties themselves or their representatives. A judge does not attend the deposition and will rule on objections later when issues are presented by the parties.

Depositions are extremely common in lawsuits. To set the stage, the questions in the deposition excerpt below asked about the witnesses' knowledge concerning a demand for payment, a relatively simple thing.

Note that the client for the overly-aggressive lawyer realizes there is a problem, and after being denied a recess, uses the excuse of having to take a bathroom break in order to speak to his out-of-control lawyer. [Omissions are not noted in the quoted text, and the identity of Attorney #1 is masked to extend some professional courtesy]:

ATTORNEY #1: Hold on. You've burned another bridge. We're not getting into that.

ATTORNEY #2: [Looking at the Witness] So you are not going to answer the question?

ATTORNEY #1: This is why this is so ludicrous it's laughable: You sent the e-mail saying $10.3 million. Why did you send that e-mail demanding $10.3 million? And now you want to quiz him on whether he was worried about that.

ATTORNEY #2: Yes.

ATTORNEY #1: It doesn't matter. You sent it. He's not going to answer why you did what you did. You still have your hand out. And until you do, it's going to smacked down. So that's the end of this.

ATTORNEY #2: [Ignoring Attorney #1, looking at Witness] So you took the $10.3 million as a credible --

ATTORNEY #1: You sent it. Are you not a credible lawyer? Are you, honest to God, asking him that question? You sent the e-mail. Now you want to say, oh, that was a joke.

ATTORNEY #2: [To Attorney #1] You need to calm down.

ATTORNEY #1: No. You need to grow up and you need to quit asking questions that are ridiculous.

ATTORNEY #2: We're not going to get personal about this.

ATTORNEY #1: Oh, kicking me out of the --

THE WITNESS: Why don't we take a brief break?

ATTORNEY #2: No, no, no. Let's continue.

ATTORNEY #1: Let's not take a break. Let's keep going. This is ridiculous. I will stand in front of the Court and say the same thing. You sent an e-mail making a demand and now you're asking him did he take it seriously.

THE WITNESS: I personally need a bathroom break. Do you mind if we do that?

In doing everything possible to avoid having his client answer questions, Attorney #1 has opened himself and his client up for sanctions. After the break, the Witness would be only too happy to respond to questions to get through the very painful ordeal of testifying with his out-of-control lawyer at his side.

After years of trial work (we've taken over 150 cases to trial), we've seen just about everything, and handled every kind of personality. Hemingway called it "grace under pressure," and despite obstacles, we provide litigation strategies that work in the real world.

First, a little more about why depositions are taken. (See Stilp, T., "A Model Letter to Witnesses," 82 Ill. Bar Journal 441). Fundamentally, lawyers take depositions to discover what a witness knows and to preserve testimony for trial. If you are ever in a lawsuit, you would be deposed for the following reasons:

1. To discover what you know about the case — the opposing attorney is searching for evidence.
2. To find evidence favorable to the other side. To this end, the opposing

attorney may attempt to maneuver you into making statements against your interest.

3. To commit you to statements under oath. If you testify under oath in your deposition that something occurred on June 1, 1994, and you attempt to change your testimony later, the opposing attorney can read that portion of the deposition at the trial, thereby using your deposition testimony against you.

4. To discredit your testimony or the testimony of other witnesses through you.

We pick up with another excerpt from that deposition testimony. [Omissions are not noted in the quoted text, and the identity of Attorney #1 is masked to extend some professional courtesy]:

ATTORNEY #1: Objection to the question. The court order stands and speaks for itself. You know it and I know it. So the fact of the matter is there's no relevance to this. You're just wasting time.

ATTORNEY #2: Well, it's my time to waste.

ATTORNEY #1: Wah, wah, wah, wah. So you had these at the ready just in case, just in case, huh? In case I got out of line, you were going to slap me with these? Go ahead. Ouch. Stop. You're hurting me.

ATTORNEY #2: Counsel, I wouldn't characterize it that way. I find that to be an unprofessional characterization.

ATTORNEY #1: I'm very unprofessional.

ATTORNEY #2: Thank you for your testimony, putting that clearly, but I'm asking the witness. [The questioning returns to get facts from the witness.]

In doing everything possible to avoid having his client answer questions, Attorney #1 has opened himself and his client up for sanctions (even with the odd admission that he is "very unprofessional").

After years of trial work (we've taken over 150 cases to trial), we've seen just about everything, and handled every kind of personality. Ultimately, the successful attorney keeps on the road, getting to the destination without embarrassing theatrics.

As a final statement on settlements, the following is based on a composite of dozens of settlement conferences, demonstrating why it is often better for the parties themselves to try to resolve their dispute rather than place the matter in the hands of a third-party.

For years, the Cook County Circuit Court was the largest unified court system in the world. Billions of dollars are at stake in its courtrooms every year.

Most lawsuits are settled out of court, many of them on the eve of trial after years of preparation. Many familiar with the system reluctantly accept the idea of spending a huge amount of time and money preparing for trials that do not happen as a necessary evil.

Somewhere between the filing of a lawsuit and the day of trial, the parties will be encouraged to discuss "settlement," and wherever the case is in its development, there will be some kind of settlement discussion.

For purposes of illustration, a settlement conference with the Judge might go something like this (based on a composite of real-life cases -- as some will note, Illinois repealed the Structural Work Act which forms the basis of this account, but is used here to avoid any comparison with actual cases):

> The lawyers enter the judge's chambers. "Sit down, fellas," said the judge, as she leaned back in her leather chair. "What have we got, a tort case?"
>
> "Yes, judge," said the plaintiff's lawyer. "A Structural Work Act claim."

"Can this be settled?"

"Judge, I'm always interested in settling cases, but I haven't heard anything from the defendant."

"Your Honor," the defendant's attorney replied, "I don't think it's incumbent on me to bid against a number I've never heard."

"You're right," said the judge. "Let me first hear what this case is about – keep it short, Counsel."

"Your Honor, my client is a 39-year-old steel worker with Otis Elevator. While working at the 225 Madison Building, he fell one floor down the elevator shaft and broke his back. The shaft opening lacked proper lighting and guard rails required by OSHA [Occupational Health and Safety Administration]. He's had two operations and hasn't been able to work since."

"What do you say?" the judge asked the defense attorney.

"I'll concede that the situation is grave, Your Honor."

"All right," said the judge, turning to the plaintiff's lawyer, "what's your demand?"

"Well . . ." the plaintiff's lawyer's voiced trailed off.

"Listen," said the judge. "I want a demand. Let's see what we can work with here."

"Judge, my client will take, today only, $1.2 million."

"That doesn't seem terribly out of line," said the judge. "Can you meet it?"

"Judge," the defense attorney began, "I'm sorry, but at this time, I don't have that kind of authority."

"Look," said the judge, "if you guys don't settle this thing, you'll be tied up two weeks in a jury trial. And I don't think I have to reminder you, counsel," the judge said looking straight at the defense attorney, "that you're in Cook County, and the juries here are pretty generous."

"Judge, I think there is still a question of liability."

"Fine," said the judge. "You've got some complicated issues here. But you know how juries are. The more cases are tried before me, the more I think juries don't understand the cases, or follow the instructions I give them. A jury could come back with a verdict many times what the plaintiff is demanding here . . ."

And on it goes. The judge speaks of the uncertainties of time, expense, and cost of litigation. To avoid this parade of horribles, the judge will say, the parties should settle.

The settlement conference highlights several common problems: (1) the judge was unfamiliar with the case; (2) the attorneys appeared without their clients, and one attorney did not even have settlement authority; and (3) the parties may have had unrealistic expectations that the judge did not, or could not, address.

A good attorney will know how to make a settlement conference effective, productive and far more likely to result in the resolution of the case. Settlements save money. Litigation stops when the parties settle. The parties are more likely to comply with the terms of a negotiated agreement than terms imposed by a court.

IV

THE PAPERWORK: PROFIT MAKING CLAUSES FOR THE BUYER

Let's assume that having read the preceding sections, the buyer finds the right property, runs the numbers, negotiates preliminary terms through a letter of intent and intermediaries, and is now ready to put together a contract. The following sections discuss first a contract with several profit-making clauses for the buyer, next, different forms of purchase for creative financing, and finally, a comparison of various forms of property ownership.

From a legal standpoint, a transfer of real estate invokes centuries of law. Historically, following the Dark Ages (from 500 to 1,000 A.D.), to transfer property, the seller and buyer would stand on the property, and the seller would throw a clump of dirt at the buyer in a ceremony known as "livery of seisin" to mark the passing of the property from one person to another. These days, the buyer and seller still attend a formal "closing," but instead of throwing dirt, that "deed" is accomplished by a transfer of paper wherein the seller and buyer exchange money for a piece of paper, a deed, to the property. The deed is the primary document that proves the transfer of a property.

Today, in more impersonal economic markets, the deed is preceded by a contract. The expression "there is no deal until money changes hands" reflects the simplicity of any real estate transaction but ignores the intricacy of the accomplishment embodied by the contract. The contract is mistakenly seen by investors as a formality to be worked out among lawyers rather than as the central document to the transaction that will define the rights and responsibilities of the seller and buyer.

The contract is an agreement that identifies the conditions of exchange, when everything is translated in to a common currency. Without a common currency, it would be difficult to answer value questions, such as "Do forty hours of labor equal two week's worth of groceries?" In this example, by translating both labor and groceries into dollar equivalents, a satisfactory exchange may be worked out. Simply put, a fair exchange is defined by a common currency that is memorialized in a contract.

Based on the fundamental belief in freedom of contract and honoring the legal intentions of competent contracting parties, the law evinces an almost sacred concern for the protection of the integrity of a written contract. Contracts provide a fascinating interplay between the public and private arenas. Essentially private agreements, contracts create value for the parties. People adhere to agreements because their adherence develops a reputation for trustworthiness and avoids the value-redistributing effects of lawsuits. Nonetheless, people may breach contracts when it is value maximizing to do so. When contracts are breached, the parties move to the courts for public enforcement of their otherwise private agreement.

Because contracts can be publicly enforced, contracts have become central to a private ownership economy. The philosophical foundations of a contract include social values, the sanctity of promises, and the right of individuals to enter into autonomous transactions consistent with democratic notions of self-government. The United States is a great experiment in self-government, seen in the contracts people write every day. Few countries in the world allow private citizens to create their own agreements then call upon the government to enforce them. Here, anyone who is a party to a contract may go to the government—that is, the court—and ask for help in enforcing the terms of a private agreement reached with another individual. A private agreement is enforced by a decision of the court, which then carries the court's support and imprimatur. And once the private contract becomes a decision of a court, the contract (or that part of it under decision) has the force of law, and the presumption is that it will be obeyed and enforced.

Although a breach of a contract may appear to lead to public consequences, the evolution of the contract has replaced the harsher reality of an earlier time. In ancient civilization, the breach of responsibility in what would be, in today's world, a construction contract or services contract, called for immediate and severe punishment to serve as a warning for others, as these rules from ancient Babylon demonstrate:

> The mason who builds a house which falls down and kills the inmate shall be put to death.

> If a man's child has died under the care of the nurse, and the nurse has substituted another (nurse) without the consent of his father and the mother [that is, breached the contract], the breasts of that nurse shall be cut off.[1]

In the present day, if one party to the contract is unwilling to abide by the terms of the agreement, the government, through the courts, may be called upon to aid in the enforcement of the contract. The parties may stipulate to damages or reparations as the cost for a breach of their agreement. Recognizing the power an individual may have through a real estate contract, the buyer should not ignore this central document to the transaction.

Preparing a real estate contract, there are two mistakes a buyer makes: (1) the buyer assumes there is only one "form" of real estate contract, and (2) the "form" has to be provided by the seller (or in most cases, the seller's broker). But there is never one "form" of contract. The buyer can put into a contract virtually any terms, limited by the buyer's imagination and what, of course, the seller is willing to accept (and for enforcement, what the law will allow). It is far better for the buyer to submit the contract and let the seller negotiate the terms that should be taken out rather than the other way around—have the buyer use the seller's contract and attempt to get terms put in. Although the buyer may save attorney's fees by allowing the seller to prepare the contract, fees are a small fraction of the price of the buyer's total investment. The buyer is penny-wise and pound-foolish to ever allow the seller to provide the "form" of the contract.

In the Appendix is a sample real estate sale agreement used on several real estate transactions. The four most important terms in the real estate sale agreement for the buyer are the following: (1) Information concerning the income, expenses, and cash flow on the property, (2) information concerning the condition of the property, (3) buyer costs to close the transaction, and (4) buyer remedies if the seller fails to perform or has given the buyer incorrect information. We will discuss each of these terms in seriatim.

A

Information Concerning the Income, Expenses and Cash Flow of the Property

The buyer may obtain information about the income, expenses, and cash flow of the property in two ways: (1) inspection of the seller's books and records, and (2) the seller's statements (representations and warranties) about the income generated by the property contained in the contract.

1. Document Inspection

The operating records for the property are a good source of information for the buyer. The seller's documents are generally truthful because the seller uses the same records in the operation of the property. These records were not necessarily created for the sale of the property and can be quite revealing. Put differently, records made in the ordinary course of business in the seller's regularly conducted business activity are, in theory, accurate and reliable because the seller depends on those very records for the seller's important undertakings in operating the property.

The buyer should request the following documents: Current Rent Roll, leases, tenant credit files, records of repairs, and the seller's tax returns.

For the more hearty readers, particular terms of the contract that may be of interest are quoted at length:

> *Documents to be furnished by seller.* Unless previously provided, within fourteen (14) days from the day of this agreement, seller shall furnish to purchaser, or make available to purchaser at a reasonable time and place for inspection, the following documents, lists, and schedules, which, together with any such documents previously delivered, are hereby certified by seller as being true, accurate, and complete:
>
> A. A current rent roll, and any rent rolls for the last two (2) years, which include a list of all units of the building, the names of all tenants occupying each unit, the expiration dates of all leases, the rental for each unit, the names of any guarantors of the leases, the amount of advance rentals and security deposits received from each tenant, and any rentals which are in arrears; a current rent roll shall also be provided within forty-eight (48) hours before closing.
> B. True and correct copies of all leases for any portion of the property (the "leases").
> C. All tenant credit files.
> D. All records of repairs or improvements made to the property since the seller's ownership of the property.
> E. True and correct copies of all management, leasing, maintenance, service, and other contracts, licenses, and equipment leases affecting the property.
> F. A copy of the most recently paid tax bill for the property, or other document showing the amount of such bill.
> G. Seller's last two (2) year's Schedule E income tax returns for the property (seller may redact information unrelated to the property).
> H. A list of all persons employed by seller in connection with the management and maintenance of the property not disclosed in paragraph E above, which list shall show all compensation and benefits such persons may be entitled to receive.
>
> *Review of documents:* The agreement is contingent upon seller's delivery to purchaser within fourteen (14) days from the date of the agreement of the documents and materials set forth above. In the event purchaser is not satisfied in its sole

discretion with its review of the documents (or the documents were not produced or made available), purchaser shall have the right to cancel this agreement.

The seller should have most of the documents available from the day-to-day operation of the property. The seller certifies the accuracy of the information provided to the buyer. An updated Rent Roll is required prior to Closing to ensure there has not been any material change in the tenancy, and prior Rent Rolls (for example, two years' worth) give the history of vacancy and collection losses (also called economic and physical vacancy). Credit files and leases will confirm the credit worthiness of tenants and the type of tenancy the buyer is purchasing (month-to-month or one-year leases). A record of improvements helps the buyer understand the scope and cost of prior maintenance. In addition, the seller's records allow the buyer to double-check that any large capital improvements were undertaken with valid permits and by qualified tradesmen. The record of repairs may be limited in time (for example, the last two years) or scope (such as all repairs costing in excess of $1,000). The seller's tax returns are a fertile source of information because to minimize taxes, the seller is unlikely to exaggerate income or underreport expenses. Usually, the seller will be conservative in the reporting of income and will zealously report every expense for deductions, thus giving the buyer the worst-case scenario of income and expenses.

2. Seller Representations and Warranties Concerning Cash Flow and Leases

In addition to a review of documents, the buyer would want the seller to make certain representations and warranties about the income and leases for the property. Although representations and warranties may cover many items, such as the physical condition or title of the property, just as to leases alone, seller representations and warranties might include the following:

> *Representations as to leases.* With respect to each of the tenants listed on the rent roll provided to purchaser by seller (the "tenants"), seller represents and warrants to purchaser

that the following are true as of the contract date and shall be true as of the closing date (and the ongoing truth of each of the following shall be a condition precedent to purchaser's obligation to close).

A. Existing leases are to be assigned to purchaser at closing, none of which will expire later than two years from the contract date, and such leases have no option to renew, cancel, or purchase.
B. The present annual gross rental income is at least $[fill in amount].
C. Each of the leases is in full force and effect strictly according to the terms set forth therein and in the rent roll, and has not been modified, amended, or altered in writing or otherwise without notice to purchaser. Each tenant is required to pay all sums and perform all obligations set forth in the leases, without concessions, abatements, offsets, or other bases for relief or adjustment.
D. All obligations of the seller as lessor under the leases that accrue to closing have been performed including, but not limited to, all required tenant improvements, cash or other inducements, rent abatements or moratoria, installations and construction (for which payment in full has been made in all cases), and each tenant has unconditionally accepted lessor's performance of such obligations. No tenant has asserted any offsets, defenses, or claims available against rent payable by it or other performance or obligations otherwise due from it under any lease.
E. No tenant is in default by more than ten (10) days or is in arrears in the payment of any sums required of it under its lease.
F. Seller has no reason to believe any tenant is, or may become, unable or unwilling to perform any or all of its obligations under its lease.
G. No guarantor(s) of any lease has been released or discharged, voluntarily or involuntarily, or by operation of law, from any obligation under or in connection with any lease or any transaction related thereto.
H. There are no brokers' commissions, finders' fees, or other charges payable or to become payable to any third party

not already disclosed on behalf of seller as a result of or in connection with any lease.
I. Each security deposit under each lease shall be fully assigned to purchaser at the closing. No tenant or any other party has or may asset any claim (other than for customary refund at the expiration of a lease) to all or any part of any security deposit.

The buyer is purchasing the cash flows of the property. Existing leases reflect current cash flow. Thus, the leases must be a fair and accurate representation of the expected income for the property. The seller's representations and warranties afford the buyer some assurance the leases are not subject to side deals, under-the-table concessions, or secret agreements between the seller and any tenant.

B

Information Concerning the Condition of the Property

Similar to information concerning the income, expenses and cash flow of the property through an inspection of records and seller's statements in the contract, the buyer may *obtain* information about the *condition* of the property in two ways: (1) a physical inspection of the property, and (2) seller's statements in the contract.

1. Physical Inspection

There is no substitute for a physical inspection of the property. Given the size of the investment, the buyer should have a trained inspector accompany the buyer throughout the property. The buyer wants access to each unit, the roof, and the basement. The seller will be required to notify all tenants of the inspection to allow entry to all units.

The inspection of a large building may take several days. The inspection will probably be the only opportunity the buyer will ever have to see the entire building at one time, assuming the buyer wants to attend all inspection days.

The inspection clause of the contract should provide the buyer with reasonable time to inspect the property, time for a written report from the inspector, and time to notify to the seller of any problems:

> *Inspection of property contingency.* Seller shall permit purchaser and its agents, at reasonable times and upon reasonable advance notice to seller, to enter upon the property, at purchaser's sole cost and expense, for the purpose of conducting such physical inspections as purchaser may elect to make or obtain. Purchaser shall indemnify and hold seller harmless with respect to any damage or injuries to persons that may result from the inspections provided for in this paragraph, whether or not the transaction contemplated by this agreement closes.
>
> Purchaser shall have a period of forty-five (45) days from the date of this agreement to notify seller in writing of any matter arising out of purchaser's investigation of the property pursuant to this paragraph. If the results of such investigations are not satisfactory to purchaser, or the property to be conveyed hereunder is not suitable for purchaser's intended use or purpose, purchaser may, on written notice to seller within such forty-five (45) day period, cancel the agreement. If purchaser does not deliver a written notice of cancellation to seller within the forty-five (45) day period, the contingency provided for in this paragraph then shall be terminated or deemed waived.

The inspection contingency gives the buyer carte blanche to get out of the deal if "the results of such investigations are not satisfactory to purchaser, or the property to be conveyed hereunder is not suitable for purchaser's intended use or purpose." The buyer has a free look at the property without any obligation to purchase. The only objection raised to the inspection contingency by most sellers is the forty-five-day period. The seller will ask to limit the contingency to thirty, twenty-one, or fourteen days, which may be acceptable if a shorter period works for the buyer.

The inspection contingency clause should be coupled with an absolute right to a refund of the buyer's earnest money to guarantee the buyer does, in fact, receive a free look:

> *Contingency period.* Any money, earnest money, or deposit shall be held by [designate a neutral, such as a title company] for the benefit of both parties and shall be immediately returned or refunded to purchaser without further consent, authorization, or direction from seller, upon written notice canceling the agreement sent by purchaser within forty-five (45) days from the date of the agreement to seller or seller's attorney, and seller hereby absolutely and irrevocably authorizes and consents to the return or refund mentioned in this paragraph without seller's further authorization, agreement, or consent needed.

In light of the inspection contingency, it is only fair the buyer have a clear right to a return of any earnest money. If the seller is reluctant to allow the buyer a full refund of earnest money *within* the contingency period (here, forty-five days), the buyer should question providing *any* earnest money.

Perhaps a few words about earnest money would be appropriate. Conventional practice requires the buyer to deposit earnest money at 5%, 10%, or 20% of the purchase price. The property, however, may be purchased without any earnest money. In one deal, a million-dollar property was bought without a single dollar paid until closing. While the lack of earnest money may make the seller, the seller's attorney, and listing broker nervous, the parties may agree in their contract that there will be no earnest money by not requiring any payment from the buyer until closing.

If the buyer agrees to provide earnest money, the buyer should never pay any money until a contract is signed. Again, conventional practice requires the buyer to pay *some* amount with the buyer's initial offer as a token of good faith. But without a contract, the buyer turns money over without knowing who will hold the money, how long the money will be held, whether the money will earn interest, and under what circumstances the money will be returned. There is no reason to leave these questions to guesswork when the contract can specify this:

> *Earnest money.* Initial earnest money of $ [amount] in the form of a check shall be held by [designate a neutral] to be paid within five (5) business days after seller's acceptance of this contract. Earnest money shall be deposited in an interest bearing federally insured account with interest to accrue for

the benefit of purchaser in compliance with the terms of this agreement.

An interesting alternative to the immediate deposit of earnest money is the "reverse-play" deposit. Instead of requiring the buyer to take affirmative steps to terminate the contract before forty-five days has passed, in the "reverse-play," the contract automatically terminates on the forty-fifth day unless the buyer sends notice to continue the contract or deposits the earnest money. For example, a contract using the "reverse-play" would simply state:

> To continue with the transaction under this Agreement, Purchaser shall deposit the sum of $XXX,XXX within three days of [a date certain, such as the Inspection Period, Due Diligence or delivery of survey], and in the absence of such deposit, the parties may assume this Agreement is null and void and shall be deemed terminated automatically without further notice to, action by, or recourse against, either party.

2. Seller Representations and Warranties Concerning Condition of Property

In addition to a physical inspection, the other source of information about the condition of the property will come from the seller. Seller representations and warranties in the contract help the buyer know what the buyer is getting. After all, the seller knows what the seller is getting: the purchase price. The buyer, however, is getting a complex asset; and who better to ask about the qualities of that asset than the person who owns it.

As shown in the sample rider to real estate sale contract, certain terms concerning the condition of the property may be placed in the general "provisions" section of the contract:

> Seller represents and warrants that the heating, plumbing, electrical, central cooling, ventilating systems, appliances, and fixtures on the premises are in working order and will be so at the time of closing, and that the roof is free of leaks and will be so at the time of closing. Purchaser shall have the

right to inspect the premises during the forty-eight (48) hour period immediately prior to closing to verify that such are in working order and that the property is in substantially the same condition, normal wear and tear excepted, as of the date of this agreement.

Seller further represents and warrants that seller has not received notice from any city, village, or other governmental authority of any yet uncured building or dwelling code violation. If seller receives such notice prior to the date of closing, seller shall promptly notify purchaser of such notice.

These paragraphs serve two functions. First, the buyer has the right to reinspect the property just before closing to ensure there has not been any material change in the condition of the property. A quick inspection minimizes any surprises after closing. Second, these paragraphs are put in another part of the contract as a backup for the central portion of the contract containing seller representations and warranties (discussed below). Although some seller representations and warranties are modified or deleted during negotiations, it is unusual that both the general provisions and seller representations and warranties portions of the contract are completely modified or deleted. In dozens of field tests involving actual real estate transactions, typically one set of seller representations and warranties or the other remains intact. Thus, the redundant provisions complement or may even stand in lieu of other provisions that are later deleted.

The bulk of the seller representations and warranties are contained in the following provisions:

Seller's representations. Seller represents to purchaser that the following matters are true as of the date of the execution of the contract and this rider (the "contract date") and shall be true as of the date of the closing of the transaction contemplated hereunder (the "closing date"):

A. *Title.* Seller is the legal fee simple titleholder of the property and has or will at closing have good, marketable, and insurable title to the property, and if a land trust is involved, seller represents that seller is the sole owner of the beneficial interest in the trust and has the authority to exercise the power of direction under the trust and is not subject to any restrictions on the exercise thereof. There are no judgments against the seller, there are no citation proceedings or other proceedings pending against the seller, which may be a charge or encumbrance against the beneficial interest in the trust.

B. *Physical condition.* There are no existing patent or latent physical defects or deficiencies in the condition of the property that would or could impair or impose costs upon the use, occupancy, or operation of the property that have not been fully corrected, and any improvements made by seller were completed and installed in accordance with all governmental authorities having jurisdiction thereover and do not violate any laws, ordinances, rules, or regulations.

C. *Utilities.* To the best of seller's knowledge, all water, sewer, gas, electric, telephone, drainage, and other utility equipment, facilities, and services for the property are installed and connected pursuant to valid permits, are adequate to service the property, and are in good operating condition and repair. Seller has not been notified of any condition that would or could result in the termination or impairment of the furnishing of service to the property of water, sewer, gas, electric, telephone, drainage, or other such utility services.

D. *Litigation.* There is no pending (or to the best of seller's knowledge, threatened) litigation, nor has there been any notice, complaint, or claim regarding the property of which seller is aware, nor are there proceedings in which seller is or may be a party by reason of any ownership or operation of the property, including building code, environmental, or zoning violations, or claims for personal injuries or property damage alleged to have occurred on the property, or, by reason of the condition, use of, or operations on, the property. No bankruptcy proceedings are pending, or to the best of seller's knowledge, threatened against seller, nor are any insolvency, bankruptcy, reorganization, or other proceedings contemplated by seller. In the event any of the foregoing is initiated or threatened prior to closing, seller shall promptly advise purchaser thereof in writing.

E. *Insurance.* Seller will maintain in force until the closing date casualty and liability insurance relating to the property and seller's assets to be conveyed hereunder. Seller has not received notice from any insurance carrier, nor is seller aware of any defects or inadequacies in the property that, if not corrected, could or would result in termination of insurance coverage or increase the normal and customary cost.

F. *Personal property.* All personal property located in, on, or around the property to be conveyed by a bill of sale is in good and operable condition and repair and free of defects.

G. *Real estate taxes.* Seller has not received notice of and does not have any knowledge of any proposed increase in the assessed valuation of the property, or such other information, which would or could effect an increase in real estate taxes.

H. *Easements and other agreements.* Seller is not in default in complying with the terms and provisions of any of the covenants, conditions, restrictions, rights-of-way, or easements affecting the property.

I. *Environmental.* The property is now owned and operated in compliance with all state, federal and/or local environmental laws, regulations, and ordinances, including but not limited to the Resource Conservation and Recovery Act, the Comprehensive Environmental Response, Compensation, and Liability Act, the Illinois Environmental Protection Act, and all laws and regulations governing underground storage tanks, asbestos, and lead-based paints.

J. *Contracts.* There are no contracts of any kind relating to the management, leasing, operation, maintenance, or repair of the property, except the documents delivered or furnished and made available to purchaser.

Again, the contract contains redundant provisions. The seller representations and warranties concerning the condition of the property overlap. If one provision is deleted, another may remain, intact or with modification, still offering the buyer assurances about the condition of the property.

If the seller is unwilling to make certain representations and warranties, the buyer should question why. For example, if the seller truly does not know whether the property is in compliance with environmental laws, the contract should be limited "to the best of seller's knowledge, the property is now owned and operated in compliance with all state, federal, and local environmental laws." Alternatively, the contract may specify "the seller has no knowledge whether the property complies with environmental laws" and allow the buyer an opportunity to investigate further with an environmental specialist who may know about asbestos or lead-based paints. Either way, the buyer is put on notice to investigate further.

The seller representations and warranties are followed with additional statements by the seller concerning the condition of the property:

> *Additional conditions precedent to closing.* The following shall be additional conditions precedent to purchaser's obligation to close:
>
> A. *Physical condition.* The physical condition of the property shall be substantially the same on the closing date as on the day of the contract date, reasonable wear and tear excepted.
> B. *Real estate taxes.* As of the closing date, there shall have been no actual or pending reassessment of the value of the property for the purpose of calculating real estate taxes of which buyer has not been previously made aware.
> C. *Utilities.* On the closing date, no moratorium or proceeding shall be pending or threatened affecting the availability, at regular rates and connection fees, of sewer, water, electric, gas, telephone, or other services or utilities servicing the property.
> D. *Operation of property.* Seller shall continue to operate and manage the property in a first-class manner, maintaining present services, including pest control, and shall maintain the property in good repair and working order, doing such work as is necessary or advisable, and as would have been done had the property not been placed under the contract and this rider for sale.
> E. *Preclosing expenses.* Seller has paid or will pay in full prior to closing all bills and invoices for labor, goods, material, and services relating to any alterations, installations, decorations, and other work for the period prior to the closing date. Except for those items for which purchaser has received a credit hereunder, purchaser has not agreed to, and will not assume, pay, perform, or otherwise discharge any debts, obligations, and liabilities of seller.

The buyer may complain all the seller representations and warranties only work if the buyer really knows how the property will operate. The buyer will not really know how the property operates until the buyer has spent several months running the property. The buyer's criticism is a valid one and may be addressed by a survival of warranties clause in the contract:

> *Survival of warranties.* The representations, warranties, agreements, covenants, and indemnities of seller set forth in the agreement or made pursuant to the agreement shall remain in full force and effect regardless of any investigation made by or on behalf of purchaser and shall survive the closing and delivery of the deed pursuant to the agreement.

The survival of warranties clause requires the seller's representations and warranties to continue past closing. In effect, the seller's statements in the contract act like insurance, protecting the buyer from any bad condition in the property the buyer did not discover until after closing. Given the potential for problems, a smart seller will delete the survival clause or limit it, for example, to six months after closing.

C

Buyer Costs to Close the Transaction

The purchase price is the single largest cost the buyer will incur to acquire a property. There are numerous miscellaneous costs, however, that in the aggregate will cost the buyer thousands. For example, in the City of Chicago, there is a transfer tax charged when a property is bought or sold. The parties may agree, between each of them, who will be responsible for certain closing costs. The contract may require the seller to pay certain costs, including the transfer tax:

Prorations and adjustments. The following shall be prorated and adjusted between seller and purchaser as of the closing date:

A. The amount of all security and other tenant deposits and interest due thereon, if any, shall be credited to purchaser at closing. Thereafter, purchaser will be solely responsible for the security and tenant deposits, and purchaser agrees to indemnify and hold seller harmless from all claims by current tenants relating to the security and tenant deposits transferred to purchaser at closing.
B. Purchaser and seller shall divide the cost of any escrows hereunder equally between them.

C. Water, electricity, sewer, gas, telephone, and other utility charges based, to the extent practicable, on final meter readings and final invoices.
D. Amounts paid or payable under the assigned contracts shall be prorated.
E. All accrued general real estate taxes applicable to the property shall be prorated on the basis of 110% of the most currently available tax bills for the property. Prior to or at closing, seller shall pay or have paid all tax bills that are due and payable prior to or on the closing date and shall furnish evidence of such payment to purchaser and the title company.
F. Seller will pay the cost of the title policy, the survey, water and sewer certificates, all documentary and transfer charges relating to the instruments of conveyance contemplated herein. Purchaser will pay the entire cost of all documentary recording fees required by law relating to or concerning the instruments of conveyance contemplated herein.
G. Such other items that are customarily prorated in transactions of this nature shall be ratably prorated.

For purposes of calculating prorations, purchaser shall be deemed to be in title to the property, and therefore entitled to the income therefrom and responsible for the expenses thereof, for the entire day upon which the closing occurs. All such prorations shall be made on the basis of the actual number of days of the year and month that shall have elapsed as of the closing.

A few observations may be helpful. Months after closing, tenants will look to the current owner of the property (now the buyer) for a refund of their security deposit. In the contract, therefore, the buyer receives a credit for all security deposits, which may ultimately have to be repaid to tenants with interest.

All utilities will be prorated. It is common for a property to have several months of unpaid utility bills because of the billing cycle. For example, water and sewer charges may be billed by the local municipality only twice a year. The buyer does not want to be stuck with the seller's utility bills.

Real estate taxes are a large expense and always seem to increase. In many areas, taxes are paid twice a year in arrears, meaning the current tax bill will cover only last year's taxes. The tax proration is calculated at 110% (a 10% premium) of current taxes to reimburse the buyer for the taxes owed while the seller owned the property and anticipate any increase. Alternatively, the parties may enter into a real estate tax reproration agreement that provides for an estimate of taxes at closing and a reconciliation a year later when the actual tax bill is received.

Paragraph F requires the seller to pay all transfer taxes—state, county, and local. Shifting the burden of closing costs to the seller in not unreasonable considering the seller is in the best position to pay closing costs after receiving the sale proceeds. The buyer may be financially strapped and will be looking for ways to save money.

D

Buyer Remedies If Seller Fails to Perform or Has Given Incorrect Information

The buyer now has the property under contract, has completed the physical inspection and reviewed the seller's records. What does the buyer do if the buyer discovers a problem? What if there are underground storage tanks or another environmental issue? What if leases are subject to tenant improvements that were supposed to be paid by the landlord and have not be completed? What if half of the refrigerators in the apartments do not work? Any of these events will constitute a breach of the seller's representations and warranties. The buyer's investigation and the seller's warranties and representations will be meaningless unless there is a built-in enforcement mechanism in the contract. And there is, as we discuss below.

The buyer's remedy for a breach of seller representations and warranties is stated in the default clause of the contract:

Default.

    A. *Default by seller.* If any of seller's representations contained herein shall not be true or correct, or if seller shall have failed to perform, or failed to perform within the time for performance as specified herein (including seller's obligation to close), purchaser may elect either to (1) terminate purchaser's obligations under this agreement by written notice to seller, and purchaser shall retain all rights and remedies available to it, including the right to a return of any money, deposit and/or consideration paid, or (2) close, in which event purchaser may deduct from the purchase price or other amounts due seller the cost of any default that remains uncured, and all reasonable expenses incurred by purchaser, including but not limited to attorneys' fees of purchaser. The remedies of purchaser set forth in this paragraph shall be in addition to remedies otherwise applicable or provided in the agreement or otherwise available to purchaser at law or in equity. All time periods in this agreement shall be tolled upon any default by seller, and shall not resume until such defaults have been fully cured.

B. *Default by purchaser.* In the event purchaser defaults in its obligations to close the purchase of the property, then seller's sole and exclusive remedy shall be to keep all money paid under the agreement, the amount thereof being fixed as liquidated damages, it being understood that seller's actual damages in the event of such default are difficult to ascertain and that such proceeds represent the parties' best current estimate of seller's damages. Seller shall have no other remedy for any default by purchaser.

C. *Indemnity of purchaser.* Seller shall and does hereby indemnify, protect, defend, and hold purchaser harmless from and against any claims, losses, demands, liabilities, suits, costs, and damages, including consequential damages and attorneys' fees of purchaser and other costs of defense incurred, arising against, or suffered by purchaser or its assigns as a direct or indirect consequence of: (1) the breach of any representation or warranty of seller set forth in the agreement; (ii) the failure of seller to perform any obligation required by the agreement to be performed by seller, or (3) any claims, costs, threatened, or pending litigation arising from or relating to preclosing uses, operation, or ownership of the property.

The default clause encompasses a breach of any seller representations or warranties, or the seller's failure to perform or perform on time. The default clause states any default by seller will excuse the buyer from performing until the seller has fully corrected the default (for instance, if the seller fails to produce records within fourteen days or allow full access for an inspection of the building).

In case of default, the buyer may either terminate the contract and receive a full refund of any money paid, or the buyer may proceed with the transaction and set off the cost the buyer incurred (for example, the cost of the refrigerators that are not working in half the units) for any significant problems.

What happens if the buyer discovers problems after closing? Ordinarily, the buyer is out of luck. Legally at closing, the contract merges with the deed and rights under the contract are extinguished. With the survival clause, however, the seller and buyer have agreed that the seller's representations and warranties survive the closing. Thus, the buyer may have a claim against the seller for defects in the property discovered even months after closing.

The most effective way for the buyer to assert a claim against the seller is through a setoff against money due the seller. A setoff may occur when the buyer still owes the seller money, for instance, when the seller financed part of the purchase price. The contract permits a setoff against any seller financing: "Purchaser may deduct from the purchase price *or other amounts due seller* the cost of any default that remains uncured" (emphasis added). If the seller agreed to finance $100,000 of the purchase price and took back a promissory note from the buyer under which the buyer promised to pay the seller the $100,000 over time, the setoff provision allows the buyer to deduct the cost of those refrigerators that are not working against the $100,000 loan.

In contrast to the buyer remedies for a seller default, the seller's remedy for a buyer default is more limited. First, there is only one type of default by the buyer: the failure to close. Second, the seller's remedy is limited to the earnest money. The seller is not entitled to any other recovery against the buyer.

If the earnest money deposit is small, the buyer is able to limit its losses. Curiously, in those transactions in which the buyer paid no earnest money (rare, but based on an actual transaction), the seller would seem to have no remedy at all. If a buyer paid no earnest money and failed to close, a court may decide the provision is unconscionable because the seller seems to have no remedy. In the purchase of a single family home, a court may find the lack of remedy unfair but may not view the provision as skeptically in a commercial transaction. A court will assume buyers and sellers of income producing property are sophisticated investors. Between sophisticated investors, a limitation on the seller's remedy may be acceptable, because in the reasoning of the courts, the seller should have known better. In commercial transactions, courts are generally reluctant to interfere with the terms of the agreement the parties struck when the seller may later, with hindsight, wish it had another different agreement.

In the last paragraph of the default provisions, the seller agrees to indemnify the buyer. The indemnity is somewhat superfluous given the buyer's remedies under the first paragraph. The indemnity is a redundant provision but is important if other buyer remedies are modified or deleted. The indemnity provision also clarifies the seller's responsibility for preclosing uses, operation, or ownership of the property. A large apartment building may have a pending lawsuit by a tenant over return of a security deposit or an injury claim if someone slipped and fell at the property. Although insurance may cover property or personal injury claims, there is no reason the buyer should assume responsibility for these problems if they arose prior to closing. In addition, the seller is in the better position to evaluate and defend claims based on facts that occurred during the seller's ownership.

E

The Whole Contract: Integrated Provisions

The provisions in the contract work together as a system—each provision coupled with another provision like framed timbers joined together exactly to make the frame of a house, all tenons and mortises fitting to afford the most protection possible. Schematically, the provisions of the contract operate in sequence: "Information" (inspection of books and records and the property); "Insurance" (seller representations and warranties and survival of warranties); and "Payment" (remedies to buyer upon seller default and buyer indemnification):

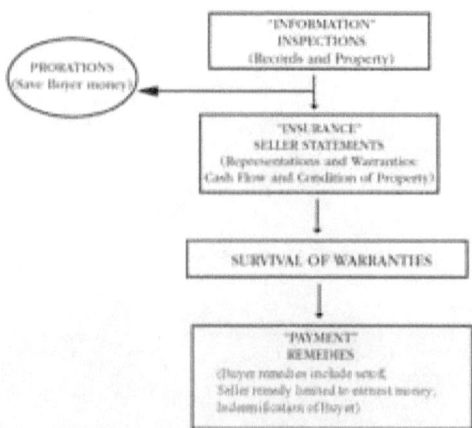

The buyer may safely assume any "form" contract offered by the seller will not contain inspections, prorations, representations, warranties, and buyer remedies. The seller's "form" contract will be missing redundant provisions that attempt to afford some protection for the buyer as the contract goes through several stages of negotiations and modifications. In the end, the buyer will be better served by investing the time, effort and money in preparing the contract.

F

Other Forms of Purchase: Alternative Financing

All of the discussion has focused on the real estate sale contract. A straight sale is one way to buy property, but there are other ways to acquire a property. The two most popular are the lease with an option to buy and the installment sale.

Both the lease-option and installment-sale contract have been called poor man's financing. Under both methods, the seller finances the property until sufficient credit is generated, either through installment payments or rent credits, to allow the buyer to pay the balance of the price or obtain a loan from another source. Both the lease-option and installment contract are delayed closing techniques. The seller retains legal title to the property until the buyer exercises the option to purchase, or until a designated time is reached in the installment sale contract and the balance of the purchase price is paid. Whichever method is used, the lease-option or installment-sale contract should include the four contract terms already discussed: (1) inspection, (2) seller representations and warranties, (3) prorations, and (4) buyer remedies. Each method is discussed in more detail below.

1. Lease with Option to Buy

The lease with an option to buy is just that, a lease with a real estate sale contract attached. The buyer may lease an entire building under a master lease. In the lease, the buyer typically assumes responsibility for paying all operating costs of the property. In exchange for rent paid to the seller and the assumption of costs, the buyer has the right to control the property and collect rents from the tenants.

The lease-option allows the buyer to lease the property from the seller and, at some predetermined time, notify the seller of the buyer's intent to purchase the property. The buyer has the exclusive right, but not the obligation, to purchase the property at the agreed-upon price (the strike price). Because the price is agreed upon in advance, a property that appreciates over time may be bought at the strike price for a bargain. On the other hand, if the property is not operating well, or declines in value, the buyer may instead allow the lease to expire and walk away without exercising the option to buy. Consequently, the lease period gives the buyer an opportunity to become familiar with the property before purchasing it.

At the heart of a lease-option is the provision setting forth the buyer's right to exercise the option to buy the property. This provision also states the amount of rent credit and the strike price to purchase the property:

> *Option.* Tenant [buyer] shall have an irrevocable option to purchase the property for a purchase price of $ on the following terms:
>
> A. Each month during the term of this agreement, the tenant shall be entitled to a credit toward the purchase price in the amount of % of each month's rent payment
> B. The $ option consideration (or deposit) paid contemporaneous with this agreement shall be credited toward the purchase price;
> C. If the option to purchase is not exercised, neither the option consideration nor any rent credit shall be refundable to tenant;
> D. The parties agree to execute the real estate sale contract attached hereto and consent to all its terms without amendment or modification, unless such amendment or modification is agreed to by both parties in writing.

Exercise of option. The option to purchase shall be exercised by written notice to the owner prior to the expiration of the option, and notice shall be provided as described in this agreement [by mail, messenger, fax].

Expiration of Option. The option to purchase may be exercised at any time during the term of this agreement and shall expire at midnight on the last day of the final term of this agreement. Upon expiration, the owner shall be released from all obligations hereunder and all of tenant's rights, legal or equitable, for the purchase of the property shall cease.

The lease-option may give the buyer a rent credit going toward the purchase price (10% to 50% of each month's rent is not uncommon). The lease-option should also contain a right to renew the lease to allow the buyer to build additional credits toward the purchase price. The seller, however, may want to limit the length of the lease and the amount of rent credited toward the purchase price. A shrewd seller will also seek a built-in escalation of the strike price to prevent a windfall to the buyer if the property significantly appreciates over time.

2. Installment Sale Contract

Like the lease-option, an installment sale contract (also called articles of agreement for deed), allows the buyer to acquire a property by making periodic payments, usually monthly, to the seller, which are credited toward the purchase price. But unlike the lease-option, which gives the buyer the right but not the obligation to purchase, the installment sale contract requires the buyer to close on the property at a definite time.

Under an installment sale, there are two closings. At the initial closing, the buyer takes possession of the property and is assigned all leases. The buyer may collect rents and operate the property. At a designated time in the contract, the buyer is required to pay the balance of the purchase price at a final closing and, at that time, the seller transfers title to the buyer by delivering the deed.

The contract buyer wants to collect the rents and apportion expenses of the property between the buyer and seller. Considering the buyer is not actually purchasing the property outright, any underlying mortgage will not be paid off. The contract buyer thus wants to be sure the seller continues to pay the underlying mortgage for the property during the term of the installment sale contract. The seller, who still holds legal title to the property, may want to continue to have tax deductions for depreciation. The installment contract should contain an assignment of rents, apportionment of expenses, and some means to ensure the underlying mortgage is being paid.

Assignment of rents. The owner assigns and transfers to purchaser (i) all the leases on the property ("leases"), (ii) all security deposits, and (iii) all the rents and revenues of the property (collectively "revenues"), authorizes purchaser or purchaser's agents, to collect the revenues and agrees that each tenant shall pay the revenues to purchaser or purchaser's agents. The purchaser shall have the right to modify, extend or terminate existing leases and to execute new leases, which in purchaser's sole discretion, are in the best interest of the property

Expenses. (a) Purchaser shall be responsible for the payment of all operating expenses for the property, including but not limited to property taxes, utilities (gas, electric, scavenger, water, and sewer), insurance, management fees, repair, maintenance, and janitor costs. The purchaser, however, is not responsible for payment of the prior mortgage (defined below), which shall be the owner's sole responsibility. (b) The owner shall have the exclusive right to all depreciation deductions for tax purposes.

Prior mortgage. The property is currently encumbered by a mortgage running from owner to [BANK] (the "prior mortgage"). The unpaid principal balance on the prior mortgage is approximately $ and the payments of principal and interest on the prior mortgage are current as of the date of this agreement. Owner shall apply a part or all of the monthly payment made by purchaser to the monthly payments on the prior mortgage until the prior mortgage is fully paid. Owner shall not further encumber the property during the term of this agreement without written consent of the purchaser.

A. Owner reserves the right to keep in place the prior mortgage against title to the property, the lien of which prior mortgage shall be prior to the interest that purchaser may have in the property, and purchaser expressly agrees upon demand to execute and acknowledge the priority of such mortgage. The prior mortgage shall not in any way accelerate the time of payment provided for in this agreement, or provide for payment of any amount exceeding the amount required under this agreement, nor shall such prior mortgage in any way restrict the right of prepayment given to purchaser under this agreement.

B. Owner shall from time to time, but not less frequently than once every three months and sooner if requested by purchaser anytime purchaser has reason to believe a default may exist, exhibit to purchaser receipts for payments made to the holder of the prior mortgage.

C. In the event the owner shall fail to make any payment required by the prior mortgage, or fail to exhibit to purchaser receipts for payments to the holder of the prior mortgage, purchaser shall have the right but not the obligation to make any such payments or cure any default under the prior mortgage and offset the amount so paid including all incidental costs, expenses and attorney's fees incurred by purchaser to protect purchaser's interests under this agreement from the unpaid balance of the purchase price and/or from any monthly installment payment to be made under this agreement.

These provisions balance the seller's and buyer's interests, apportion expenses, and make explicit the seller's obligation to pay the prior mortgage during the lease. By the way, the same provisions may be used in a lease with an option to buy contract if there is a mortgage and a concern about payment of that mortgage.

The flexibility of the installment sale is seen in this example of a seven-unit building. The building's large units, three bedrooms and one and a half bath, and six-car garage needed a lot of work. Because the buyer's available cash would be used for repairs, the buyer wanted to make a low down payment. The buyer also wanted low monthly payments. Even though the buyer successfully negotiated the price down from $279,000 to $225,000, a conventional mortgage would require a large down payment of at least 20% of the price ($45,000) and monthly payments of several thousand dollars each month at market interest rates.

The seller's underlying mortgage balance was $162,000. The seller was willing to help finance the eventual purchase of the property but did not want to give up the property without adequate security. The buyer needed to balance the buyer's need for a low down payment and low monthly payments against the seller's need for security.

The buyer suggested an installment sale. With an installment sale, the seller retained legal title so that in case of a default, the seller would have security. The terms of the final deal included the following:

- $225,000 price
- About 10% down
- $2,100 per month
- Twelve month moratorium on payments (no payments for a year)
- Seven-year balloon at which time the balance of the purchase price became due

The installment sale gave the buyer the flexibility in cash flow and gave the seller reasonable security. The seller could take part of the money paid each month, and apply it toward the underlying mortgage and pocket the difference.

In the sample installment contract, the seller must pay the prior mortgage. The contract also prohibits any other liens on the property that may adversely affect the buyer's right of ownership. Good intentions, however, are not enough. Over the years, the seller may be involved in a lawsuit that results in a lien against the property without the seller's consent, or the seller may refinance the property or attempt to sell the property to someone else. To protect its interest, the buyer should record a memorandum of agreement in the local recorder's office for the county in which the property is located. The memorandum of agreement gives notice to the world the buyer has rights in the property, and events occurring subsequent to the recordation of the memorandum will take subject to the buyer's rights. The contract need simply state this:

> *Memorandum.* Contemporaneous with the signing of this agreement, owner will sign the memorandum of agreement attached hereto, which purchaser may record with the office of the recorder of deeds.

The Memorandum itself should be signed by both parties and recorded. The Memorandum may state:

MEMORANDUM OF AGREEMENT

This memorandum of agreement is made with respect to an installment sale contract dated (the "agreement"), and by and between ("owner") and ("purchaser").

WITNESSETH:

1. Owner and purchaser have entered into the agreement concerning property legally described as [LEGAL DESCRIPTION] located in [CITY], [COUNTY], [STATE] (the "property").
2. The term of the agreement is approximately X years commencing on [DATE].
3. Pursuant to the terms of the agreement, the purchaser has an exclusive right to purchase the property.
4. No lease, mortgage, sale, transfer, lien, or other encumbrance affecting the property which is created or entered into after the date of this memorandum and prior to termination of the agreement shall be valid or effective without obtaining the prior written consent of purchaser, all such leases, mortgages, sales, transfers, liens, or other encumbrances shall be void and of no force and effect against purchaser or purchaser's interest in the property.
5. The covenants and agreements of owner under the agreement are covenants running with the land and shall be binding upon the owner and the owner's heirs, representatives and assigns.

IN WITNESS WHEREOF, the parties have caused this memorandum of agreement to be executed this [DATE] for the purpose of providing an instrument for recording.

OWNER: _____   PURCHASER: _____

A word of warning—the seller may not want to sign a memorandum of agreement because it will trigger the due on sale clause in the seller's mortgage. (The due on sale clause allows a lender to accelerate payments under the loan and declare all payments immediately due and payable upon a "sale" of a property). The memorandum of agreement is not a sale and does not jeopardize the mortgage lender's priority because the buyer expressly agreed the lender's mortgage was prior to the buyer's interest. Thus, once explained to the lender, the memorandum of agreement should not trigger the due on sale clause.

The provisions discussed here are important for the buyer. The seller, of course, will want different terms. These terms may include the buyer's obligation to keep the property (1) in good repair, (2) insured, and (3) free from liens for any work performed at the buyer's request. In addition, the seller will want (4) access to inspect the property, (5) remedies upon default (eviction of buyer, termination of the contract, and a right to collect rents upon default), (6) increase the purchase price for any costs incurred by seller because of buyer's fault, and (7) interest. Because these terms benefit the seller, they are not discussed here, but the buyer should be aware that these terms are typically included in a completed contract.

The buyer should recognize that the lower down payment used with a lease-option or installment contract may create a problem for the seller, especially with a broker's commission. Technically, a broker's commission is not earned because no sale occurred under either a lease-option or installment sale. A commission should be due only when the deed is transferred from the seller to the buyer. Nonetheless, the buyer should ask about the broker's out of pocket expenses and suggest part of the earnest money be used to pay these expenses, or part of the option consideration in a lease-option be used as a leasing commission. The balance of the broker's commission will be paid when the option to purchase is exercised, or the sale is closed.

G

Forms of Ownership

No legal discussion would be complete without mention of the forms of real estate ownership. The forms of property ownership are not just an esoteric topic of interest to lawyers but have practical consequences to the real estate investor.

There are several ways to own real estate: in the owner's name, land trust, partnership, limited partnership, C-corporation, S-corporation, and limited liability company. Here is a comparison of these common forms of ownership:

TYPE	LIMITATION ON LIABILITY	TRUE OWNER NAME HIDDEN	DOUBLE TAXATION	RESTRICTIONS
OWNER NAME	No	No	No	No
LAND TRUST	No	Yes	No	Yes
PARTNERSHIP	No	No	No	No
LIMITED PARTNERSHIP	Only as to Limited Partners	Only as to Limited Partners	No	Yes
C-CORP.	Yes	Yes	Yes	Yes
S-CORP.	Yes	Yes	No	Yes
LIMITED LIABILITY CO.	Yes	Yes	No	No

A property may be held in a person's real name under sole ownership. When title is held in this manner, there is no limitation on liability. The owner's personal assets, car, home, and bank accounts are exposed and may be seized for payment of the property's debts and liabilities. Worse, the owner's name is a matter of public record, so anyone who cares to know need only visit the local county office where deeds are recorded to find what property the owner has.

Holding property in a land trust is a little better. A land trustee (usually a local bank or title company) holds legal title. The owner is the beneficial owner of the trust. The public record will show the bank, for example, "American National Bank, as Trustee" as the owner. The trust document itself is not a public record, so the beneficiary is not known. People mistakenly believe because the owner's name is not a matter of public record, the land trust limits the owner's liability. The land trust will not protect the owner from contractual liabilities. The land trustee will not enter into agreements for utilities, repairs, maintenance, management fees, and sundry other obligations incurred in the ordinary course of the property's business. In fact, the land trustee will insist on an exculpatory clause in any document the trustee signs, stating "American National Bank, as Trustee" is not liable for any debts incurred for the property. People dealing with the property, therefore, will insist on the owner's personal signature.

A partnership is much like a property held under sole ownership, except two or more people own the property. Title itself may be held by the partners as tenants in common, joint tenants, or—in some states—tenancy by the entirety if husband and wife own the property. The partners may individually or collectively sign documents to bind the partnership, which is to say, one another.

Tenants in common, joint tenants, and tenants by the entirety are forms of joint property ownership. Joint tenants share a right of survivorship. If one joint tenant dies, that person's ownership interest passes automatically to the other joint tenant. Tenants in common do not have a right of survivorship. If one tenant in common dies, that person's interest passes to his estate and his heirs. Tenancy by the entirety exists in some states for husband and wife. The law treats the ownership of the property as a unified whole; a creditor of one spouse cannot affect the title of the property and the other spouse's interest. Of course, if one spouse dies, the tenancy by the entirety is terminated.

A limited partnership consists of one general partner and one or more limited partners. The limited partners have at risk only the amount of their investment and no personal liability. The corollary to limited liability is a severe restriction on the limited partners' ability to participate in decisions affecting the property. Generally "silent partners," the limited partners must adhere to these restrictions or they will lose their limited liability protection.

Title to real estate may be held by a C-corporation. A C-corporation offers limited liability protection and anonymity to the owners. A distinct disadvantage of the C-Corp. is double taxation. The C-corporation is taxed on its own earnings, and the company's shareholders are taxed on any distribution from the corporation. Thus, the net earnings generated by a property will be taxed at the corporate level, and any payment to the company's owners (shareholders) will be taxed at the individual level.

Like a C-corporation, a subchapter S-corporation offers limited liability protection and anonymity to the owners. The S-corporation has an advantage over the C-corporation, however, because there is no double taxation. Instead, the S-corporation is subject to many restrictions concerning the number of shareholders, types of shares, and tax penalties for excess passive income, which is typically generated by real estate.

Only the Limited Liability Company (or LLC) provides the combination of the most desirable attributes for the small real estate entrepreneur: limited liability protection, anonymity, flow-through taxation, and few restrictions. An LLC is an organization in which the owners of the LLC, called members, are not personally liable for the debts and expenses of the company. A member, like a shareholder of a corporation, owns an interest in the LLC. At the same time, a member is like a partner. An LLC member is a party to the contract known as the operating agreement that governs the internal operation of the LLC.

The LLC owners have the freedom to establish ownership, management, and operating relationships based on the operating agreement between the owners of the LLC without the rigid formalities of a corporation. Unlike a C-corporation, there is no double taxation. Gains and losses (like depreciation) flow through the LLC to the individual owners. And unlike an S-corporation, an LLC can have an infinite number or types of interests, senior interests, preferred interests, and cumulative, nonvoting, or subordinated interests. Although the LLC has advantages over the C-corporation and S-corporation, it has the common characteristic of continuity of life. The LLC does not necessarily dissolve on the dissociation of a co-owner of the LLC, like a partnership. This characteristic is useful when the LLC holds real estate, and title might be adversely affected by dissolution or any change that occurs when a partner leaves a partnership. Furthermore, the LLC enables owners to participate in decisions affecting the property without losing liability protection, and in this respect, the LLC has an advantage over limited partnerships.

The LLC may even own other LLCs or corporations. This becomes important in more complicated forms of property ownership. For example, a limited partnership may hold legal title to real estate, and an LLC may act as general partner, thus affording limited liability protection to the general partner usually absent in a traditional limited partnership:

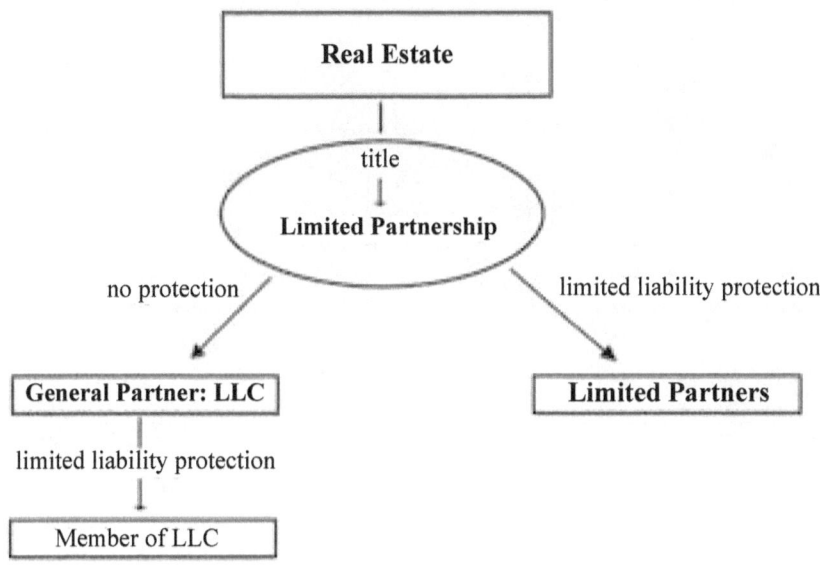

A limited partnership is another way to finance the purchase of a property. Instead of seller financing using a mortgage, the limited partnership holds the title to the real estate. The seller is given a promissory note. The seller becomes a member of the ownership entity and acts as a limited partner, with the right to collect rents in case of the buyer's default in payment under the note. The advantage of this type of financing is that it offers the seller some protection; while at the same time, it avoids encumbering the property with another mortgage, which may be a violation of loan covenants of a commercial lender who finances the balance of the purchase price.

End Notes

1. E.A. Wallis Budge, *Babylonian Life and History*, 2nd ed. (London: Religious Tract Society, 1925), pp. 128 + 130.

V

CASE STUDY

Medical students are encouraged to learn by the saying, "See one, do one, teach one." Law students review cases then are questioned by professors as to the facts and rules of law of these real-life cases under the socratic question-and -answer method. Business students analyze company strategies under the case method. The willingness to learn from the experience of others is an important determinant of success in many professions.

Students of real estate may learn from the experience of others by examining real estate transactions. The following case study reviews the strategies and techniques discussed throughout this book, which were used in an actual transaction.

A

Forty-three-unit Apartment Building for $13,500

The property in this case study was found one Sunday in the *Chicago Tribune* real estate classified ads. The property is a forty-three-unit apartment building located on the north side of Chicago, in a lower middle income area of the city. Having six two-bedroom units and thirty-seven one-bedroom units, the courtyard building is located one block from the lake, parks, the El (elevated trains) and rapid transit. The average rent is $450 per month for the one-bedroom units and $575 per month for the two-bedroom units. The property generates $221,500 gross scheduled income per year. The seller is asking $895,000, or about four times the gross rent (known as the gross rent multiplier). At the time, prices for buildings in this area of the city are typically between 3.5 to 5 times gross rent. Thus, a building with $220,000 annual gross scheduled rent may be priced between $770,000 (3.5 x $220,000) to $1,100,000 (5 x $220,000).

After some investigation, the buyer discovers the property was listed a year ago at $835,000 and taken off the market. The property had about $100,000 in capital improvements since the last listing. The current owners live in Florida (the Florida factor meaning the owners are absentee and retired) and have owned the property about twenty years. There is no mortgage on the property. The property is managed through a local real estate management company. The owners are tired of the ownership headaches, including several recent minor building code violations by the city (e.g., porches need painting and windows are missing screens).

The real estate broker sends the buyer a property brochure, a portion of which is duplicated at the end of this book. Note how the broker figures differ by 20% to 25% from the investor's initial proforma, discussed earlier in this book and reprinted here for convenience:

APARTMENT COMPLEX
43 UNITS, CHICAGO, ILLINOIS

Gross Income	228,360
Vac 6%	(13,702)
Bad Debt 1.5%	(3,425)
Other Income	1,000
Effective Gross	212,233
Operating Expenses	
Tax	(41,340)
Insurance	(5,232)
Gas	(21,000)
Electric	(2,364)
Water/Sewer	(4,120)
Scavenger	(2,700)
Maintenance	(21,500)
Payroll (Janitor)	(10,750)
Admin & Gen.	(1,500)
Exterminating	(500)
Misc.	(2,000)
Marketing	(1,982)
Management 5%	(10,612)
Reserve 5%	(10,612)
TOTAL	(136,212)
Expected NOI	76,021

Remember, the broker is trying to sell the property and will portray the property in the best light. Broker figures should be taken only as a starting point. The investor should independently confirm all figures through the seller's own books and records for the property, as well using information about the neighborhood. If the area has a chronic 6% vacancy and 1.5% bad debt, the investor should figure this vacancy / bad debt loss into the proforma, as we have done.

Because the numbers looked good, the buyer scheduled an appointment to visit the property. At the property, the buyer saw several one-bedroom apartments, and a two-bedroom apartment. The buyer also saw the basement and boiler and walked around the neighborhood. While at a property, the buyer spoke with a few tenants. How long have they lived at the building? Do they like the neighborhood? How is their apartment? Have they had any problems? Do they get enough heat during the winter? Tenants candidly tell the buyer about their experience with the property.

Within a few days of the visit, the buyer sent a letter of intent, which is reproduced at the end of this book. The letter of intent contemplates seller financing because there was no mortgage on the property. Under the letter of intent, the buyer offered $837,300, waived the 3% commission to the buyer's broker, who is in-house with the buyer, thus saving the seller $25,119 as a partial commission that would otherwise be paid to the buyer's broker as a cooperating commission. The price would be paid with $50,000 down, and the balance over eight years to the seller, quarterly, on a forty-year amortization, with interest at 8.25%, 1.25% of which would be deferred for two years. Based on information from the seller's broker, the buyer assumed, wrongly as it turned out, that the seller was not concerned about receiving a large cash payment at closing.

Two weeks later, the buyer sent a second letter of intent, also reproduced at the end of this book. In the second offer, the buyer decreased seller financing to 10% of the purchase price. This gave the seller a large cash payment at closing. The buyer also dropped the purchase price to $832,000 and insisted on a 3% commission to the buyer's broker ($24,960), thereby netting the seller $807,040. In addition, there was a six-month moratorium on any payments to the seller on the seller financing. The balance of the purchase price would be paid through bank financing and cash from investors.

In response to the buyer's second offer, the seller wanted a higher price. In exchange, the seller was willing to offer more favorable financing. About ten days latter, the buyer sent the third and final letter of intent, attached at the end of this book.

The terms of the third letter of intent were ultimately accepted by the seller. The buyer agreed to pay $851,000. The seller increased the amount of seller financing to 12.5% of the price and agreed to a moratorium on payments, *without* interest, for two years. The seller also agreed to pay a 3% commission to the buyer's broker, which could be applied as a credit toward the purchase price for the buyer.

In the next three weeks, a contract was prepared and signed. The form of the contract used appears in the appendix. The seller consented to most of the representations and warranties concerning the income and condition of the property. The seller also agreed to pay many of the closing costs, including the city transfer taxes, which alone totaled $6,382.50.

During the same month, the buyer inspected the building. The buyer hired a professional inspector for $1,500, who wrote a report the buyer showed the seller later. The inspection took a full day. The buyer went through almost every unit, the roof, basement, and inspected the major mechanical systems of the property. The buyer also reviewed the seller's books and records, tax returns, historic rent rolls, leases, and tenant credit files.

Within the forty-five-day contingency period for property inspection allowed by the contract, the buyer sent a letter to the seller, a copy of which is reproduced at the end of this book. The letter summarized the results of the buyer's inspection. The letter also raised several breaches of the seller's representations and warranties contained in the contract. The buyer requested the following from the seller: (1) cure the breaches of representations and warranties (e.g., make repairs), (2) credit the buyer with $55,000 for those breaches the seller will probably not be able to cure before closing, and (3) extend the moratorium on payments for six years on the seller financing.

After a month of negotiating, the seller agreed to credit the buyer with $70,000 (thus, the purchase price was reduced from $851,000 to $781,000), and in exchange, the buyer agreed to waive the breaches of the seller's representations and warranties and proceed with the closing. The change in price was based on a "cram down" position in the contract, which allows the buyer to set off the cost of major repairs against the purchase price. The terms of the final transaction include the following (letter attached in the appendix):

- Price: $781,000.
- Bank financing of $680,800 (the bank finances the loan based on the expected cash flow of the property and the appraised value of the property, which substantially exceed the new price).
- Seller financing of $36,375 at 8.25% interest, payable quarterly, with a two-year moratorium on payments *without* interest. The loan will balloon after six years.
- Investor financing from a third party of $25,000 at 7.5% interest, payable quarterly, amortized over thirty years. The investor also has a 33% participation in the residual value of the property upon sale over the original sale price of $851,000. This means if the property later sold for $1,000,000 net (after allowing for all costs of sale), the investor would receive the unpaid balance of the $25,000 loan, plus 33% of $149,000 ($1,000,000-$851,000), or $49,170—a sweet deal for any investor with a $25,000 loan.
- Over $50,000 in buyer credits for real estate taxes (which were not yet due but would have to be paid in the future), security deposits, utilities, earnest money, and commission. Even though the buyer paid about $13,500 out of pocket, at closing, the buyer got back $16,000 for an immediate $2,500 "profit."

The buyer took over the property with four vacancies out of forty-three units, roughly a 10% vacancy. During the first few months of property ownership, the buyer filled the vacancies. After one full year, the property generated $212,223 in revenues, and the buyer paid $145,101 in expenses, not including debt service. The buyer put in over $40,000 in capital improvements, using money the property itself generated. The buyer turned a tidy little profit of about $16,800 cash after debt service. In addition, loan amortization was about $9,000.

At 95% leverage ($680,800 bank financing + $36,375 seller financing + $25,000 investor financing / $781,000), large borrowing will not be for everybody. High debt is risky if a property has large operating expenses and unpredictable income. When a property has a more predictable cash flow, it may carry more leverage. In the buyer's case, the two-year moratorium on payments for seller financing helped ease some financial pressure in the early years of ownership.

But how can an investor get a large loan? Remember, sources of financing are interested in the cash flow of the property. Investors are buying cash flow, or more properly, assumptions about the cash flow. Leverage works best when a lender can see income from the property as the source to repay the loan. The lender is inside out when the loan amount exceeds the value of the building. If the property has cash flow, and the buyer is purchasing the property at a good price, a lender will be willing to loan money, as what happened with the buyer here.

As far as the change in the purchase price from $851,000 to $781,000, a broker protested that the seller representations and warranties were "a lot of legal mumbo jumbo." It is not a lot of legal mumbo jumbo to insist the seller comply with the terms of the agreement the seller signed. If the seller is truthful, the seller's compliance is only fair. To the contrary, it is unfair for the seller to sign an agreement, then when called upon to honor the promises contained in that agreement, protest it is "a lot of legal mumbo jumbo" just to get out of the deal.

The buyer wants the negotiations with the seller to be friendly and fair. The buyer wants to buy, and the seller wants the buyer to buy. But those who claim the buyer should make friends with the seller while negotiating have the wrong idea. Income-producing property is a business. The seller is selling to make a profit, and the buyer hopes by buying to make a profit too. If the buyer discovers something that makes the buyer believe it needs to renegotiate some of the terms, including the price, then the buyer should go back to the table.

To those who still believe postcontractual negotiations inveigle the seller out of hard-earned money, let us put the seller's representations and warranties into another context. Most buyers want assurances that the seller has a good title and is the rightful owner of the property. In the old days, and still in some small towns, lawyers search public records and give opinions on titles. In other areas, title insurance replaces the attorney's opinion about whether the seller has a good title. If there is a problem with the title after the purchase, title insurance pays the buyer for the value of the property, or the reduced value of the property for the defects in the title.

The seller usually pays for a title insurance policy before closing. Imagine if the seller was not willing to provide title insurance, or any assurance of good title. What would the buyer be willing to pay for such a property? It would depend on what the buyer could discover about the state of the title, but with no assurances of good title, the buyer would probably pay a lot less than the buyer would pay with such assurances.

The seller's representations and warranties about the condition and income of the property are like title insurance (or an attorney's opinion about good title). The contract simply defines the terms of exchange. The seller may offer to sell the property in an "as is" condition, without any representations or warranties. A property in an "as is" condition merits one price, whereas a property with representations and warranties deserves another price. A property with representations and warranties is more valuable because the seller is willing to say, "I promise the property is in such-and-such condition, the roof doesn't leak, and the mechanical systems are in good repair and working order." The seller, who may have owned the property for years, is in the best position to know. When the seller is unwilling to make any promises about the condition of the property, the buyer knows to look for possible problems. In such a case, the buyer is asked to assume responsibility for problems in return for a price adjustment to compensate the buyer for the risk. In an "as is" sale, the buyer may get stuck with any problems, and the price of the property should reflect that it was sold without warranties or representations.

In the instance of the buyer's contract in the case study, the seller made warranties and representations about the condition of the property. The representations and warranties represent qualities and characteristics of the property. The price of the property was negotiated and reflected the certain qualities and characteristics of the property. If the statements by the seller are not accurate, and the representations and warranties are not consistent with the actual condition of the property, the price is no longer accurate. Postcontractual negotiations do nothing more than align the price of the property with the reality of the property's qualities and characteristics as promised. In this case, a $70,000 reduction in price was warranted.

The next section reviews the use of leverage and cost of debt and their affect on the investor's return in the case study. The final section discusses compounding, an important but sometimes overlooked cost of a loan.

B

The Use of Leverage

The property in the case study had 95% leverage. For those interested how leverage affects return, the buyer may apply two measures: cash on cash return and return on equity.

For any given year, cash on cash return is simply the amount of money paid out of pocket divided by the cash generated by the property after debt service:

$$\text{CASH ON CASH} = \frac{\text{CASH OUT OF POCKET}}{\text{CASH AFTER DEBT SERVICE}}$$

The amount of cash generated by the property was $16,800. The amount paid out of pocket was, well, zero (remember the buyer got $2,500 back at closing). Technically, $16,800 / 0 is an infinite return and, therefore, not very helpful in this case.

Return on equity (or ROE) will be more useful here, but it is more complicated to calculate. ROE is equal to:[1]

$$\text{Return on Equity} = \frac{\text{Return on Asset - Cost of Debt}}{\text{Equity}}$$

Why calculate return on equity? The cap rate formula provided a way to compare different properties without worrying about the cost of debt. Whether there was little debt or a lot of debt, a low interest rate or high interest rate was not taken into account. ROE is a tool to measure the performance of a property *given* its debt.

Return on equity (ROE) has three elements: (1) return on asset—that is, what the buyer gets—less (2) the cost of debt—namely, how much it costs the buyer to get it—divided by (3) the amount of equity the buyer has in the property. We calculate each separately below to find ROE.

The first element, return on asset, is equal to the net operating income, i.e., what the property pays, divided by the price of the property, i.e., what it cost the investor to "buy" that income, plus an expected growth rate. Return on asset is:

Return on Asset = $(NOI_{Year1} / P_0) + g$
where: NOI = Net Operating Income for a given year
P_0 = Price
g = growth, usually the rate of inflation, assuming a 100% pass-through of inflation to rents

The return on asset calculation is nothing more than a rearrangement of the cap rate formula discussed earlier (P_0 = NOI / cap rate) with an added growth rate. Using the forty-three-unit building as an example, the buyer collected $212,223 in the first year, with operating expenses of $145,101. The buyer's NOI was $67,122 ($212,223-$145,101). The price of the property was $781,000. We assume the rate of inflation was 2.5%. Putting all the information together, the return on asset for the forty-three-unit building was this:

Return on Asset = $(NOI_{Year1} / P_0) + g$
= ($67,122 / $781,000) + 2.5%
= 8.6% + 2.5% = 11.10%

The buyer's actual return on asset of 11.1% is pretty close to the cap rate (akin to initial yield) of 11.5% the buyer estimated as a return before the buyer bought the property. (See Complex Analysis Section II (D), cap rate.)

Next, we have to determine the cost of debt. The cost of debt could be the interest rate charged by the lender. The 8.75% is the amount stated in the promissory note the buyer signed. The calculation for the cost of debt is a bit more complex, however, than the stated interest rate because the lender required the payment of points of 2% of the loan amount, or $680,800 x 2% = $13,616. The buyer did not get $680,800, but really only $667,184 ($680,800-$13,616). Even though the buyer received $680,800, the buyer first paid out of pocket $13,616, so the loan cost the buyer more than 8.75%. The effective interest rate on this loan was actually 9.18% (including compounding). This rate was found by plugging the amount of the loan proceeds received, $667,184, with the stated monthly payments required by the loan documents, $5,682, amortized over twenty-five years, also stated in the loan documents. Given three known variables, the loan amount, monthly payment, and the period of amortization, the financial calculator provides the fourth variable, the interest rate of 9.18%.

For those mathematically interested, the rate may be found by the formula imbedded in the calculator, which is:

Loan Amount = Monthly Payment $[(1 + r)^n - 1 / (1 + r)^n r]$

Given the loan amount, monthly payment, and 25 year amortization schedule, we can solve for r by interpolation, using 9% first (to know why we divide and multiply by "12," see the next Section on Compounding):

$667,184 = 5,682 [(1 + 9\%/12)^{25 \times 12} -1 / (1 + 9\% / 12)^{25 \times 12} (9\% / 12)]$

$667,184 = 677,105$

Because the right side of the equation (677,105) is too large, we will use a larger number to reduce the right side of the equation, like 9.3%, which yields:

$667,184 = 660,821$

Now, the right side is too small, so the actual percentage rate must be about midway between 9% to 9.3% which is about 9.18%.

The cost of debt is complicated further because there is not one loan on the property, but three: the bank loan of $680,800, seller financing of $36,375, and the third-party investor loan of $25,000. For simplicity, we will ignore the two-year moratorium on the seller financing (which reduces the interest rate from 8.25% to roughly 4.4%) and the 33% residual participation of the third-party investor. To determine the cost of debt, we take a weighted average of the three loans—given the stated amount of each loan, divided by the purchase price, multiplied by the interest rate of each loan—and add up the results:

$$\frac{\$680,000 \times 9.18\%}{\$781,000} + \frac{\$36,375 \times 8.25\%}{\$781,000} + \frac{\$25,000 \times 7.5\%}{\$781,000} = 8.6\%$$

The total Cost of Debt is 8.6%

The last element on the return on equity is the amount of equity the buyer has in the property. The amount of equity is found by 100% less the total debt expressed as a percentage. The asset is 100% (or 1.00). The asset is always 100% because the asset is the whole pie. Here, equity is 1-95%, or 5% (remember from the discussion above there was 95% debt). There is only 5% equity in this property, a highly leverage deal.

Having performed the three calculations necessary to find ROE, the return on the buyer's 5% equity is found by this formula:

$$\text{Return on Equity} = \frac{\text{Return on Asset - Cost of Debt}}{\text{Equity}}$$

$$= \frac{[(NOI_{Year 1} / P_0) + g] - \text{Debt}}{1 - \text{Debt}}$$

$$= \frac{11.10\% - 8.6\%}{5\%} = 50\%$$

The buyer's return on equity is 50%, a very strong return. To determine the effect of leverage, consider what would happen if we dropped all private financing, from individuals, $36,375 + $25,000 in this case, and left only the first mortgage. We need to recalculate the cost of debt. Recall the effective interest rate charged by the bank is 9.18%. But the cost of debt is not against the entire cost of the property, only $680,800/$781,000, or 87.17% of it. The weighted cost of debt is, therefore, 9.18% x 87.17%, which equals 8%. Without the private financing from individuals, the buyer would have to put more money into the property. The buyer's Equity would increase to 1-87.17%, or 12.83%. The buyer's return on equity becomes:

$$\text{Return on Equity} = \frac{11.10\% - 8\%}{12.83\%} = 24.16\%$$

The return on equity was cut in half—why? When the return on asset (11.10%) exceeds the total cost of debt (8.6%), more leverage is good. The buyer is better off making money with other people's money. The corollary of this rule is that if the cost of debt *exceeds* the return on asset, the buyer wants to reject the use of leverage because it will cost more than what the property can generate.

The high degree of leverage from a bank, 87.17%, is unusual, although many banks may be willing to go as high as 80%. Higher leverage typically entails higher cost of debt to compensate the lender for the increased possibility of a default risk. In addition, higher leverage triggers greater lender scrutiny and loan covenants generally become more restrictive, affecting the buyer's freedom to operate the property. Ultimately, the amount of leverage on a property depends on the buyer's confidence the property's return will exceed the cost of the loan and the trade-offs the buyer is willing to accept.

C

Compounding

The cost of debt increased from 8.75% to 9.18% on the first mortgage because of points. The cost of debt on the mortgage also increased because of compounding. When considering the cost of debt, a buyer needs to account for points and compounding to fairly compare one loan with another, not simply look at the stated percentage rate in the loan documents. A buyer must consider the effect of compounding on the cost of the loan.

The two factors that affect compounding are (1) time, and (2) the interest rate. Time simply measures how often interest gets added to the principal. If annual, interest is added once each year, so in the next year, the lender earns interest on the principal *plus* interest on the previous year's interest. Monthly is more frequent than annually, and daily is more frequent than monthly. The more frequent the compounding, the higher the cost of the debt. The second factor, the interest rate, is the rate stated in the loan documents before compounding. Obviously, interest will grow faster with compounding at an interest rate of 10% than 6%.

To understand the effect of compounding, look at this example. Assume a loan is $100,000 at 10% payable once per year. Without compounding, the cost of the loan is $10,000 per year ($100,000 x 10%). If the lender compounded monthly and wanted payments each month, the cost of the loan becomes $1/12^{th}$ of 10% each month (10% / 12), multiplied twelve times for the year, once for each month (10% / 12) x (10% / 12), etc., or using short-hand with exponents:

$(rate/12)^{12} = (10\%/12)^{12} = 10.47\%$

So the rate increased from 10% to 10.47% with monthly compounding. Assume the buyer was able to avoid compounding and pay the lender once a year. If the buyer invested the $100,000 at the 10% rate compounded monthly, at the year's end, the buyer would earn $100,000 x 10.47%, or $10,470 before paying the lender. The buyer would pay net to the lender $10,000, keep the $470, thus realizing an effective interest rate of 9.53%, $10,000-$470, or $9,530 / $100,000. If the situation were reversed, and compounding favored the lender (as it usually does), the lender would receive 10%, plus the $470 bonus, or .47%. The lender's effective interest rate would be 10.47%.

The general formula for compounding is this:

$\$1 (1 + rate/compounding)^{years \, x \, compounding}$

Where "compouding" is the number of compounding intervals per year. For every month:

$\$1 (1 + rate/12)^{12}$

Everyday:

$\$1 (1 + rate/365)^{365}$

And for a number of years, this becomes:

$\$1 (1 + rate/compounding)^{years \, x \, compounding}$

Compounding Interval	Final Sum	Effective Annual Rate
Once Per Year $100,000 (1+10%/1)^1$ simplifies to $100,000 (1+10%)$ or (1.10)	$110,000	10%
Monthly $100,000 (1+10%/12)^{12}$	$110,470	10.47%

Every Day $100,000 (1+10\%/365)^{365}$	$110,520	10.52%

As can be seen, compounding increases the Cost of Debt.

End Notes

1. The return on equity discussion is based on J. Pagliari, Jr. and R. Garrigan, "Leveraged Investments for Tax-Exempt Investors: The Financial Perspective," in *The Handbook of Real Estate Portfolio Management,* (Pagliari, editor, 1995), pp. 636-649.

VI

IDEAS ABOUT RUNNING A PROPERTY

The buyer has the property under contract and closes the sale. Congratulations—the buyer is now a landlord. Now the buyer must know how to manage the property. Income-producing property is a business, and residential real estate is management intensive. A large building has a staff of people: a property manager, a janitor, an assistant janitor, office personnel to handle tenant complaints and show apartments to prospective renters, and a bookkeeper to ensure rents are recorded and bills are being paid. The next sections discuss (A) why it is important to keep a fully rented building, even at below market rents, contrary to popular belief, (B) how to pay your management company right, as your partner, not as an independent contractor, (C) what you can do to get rid of your bad tenants, including rules of thumb for rent collection, evictions, and tenant screening, and (D) how to keep your good tenants as long as possible, secure tenant commitment, use tenant questionnaires, and exploit market opportunities.

A

Spreading Fixed Costs: Always Keep a Fully Rented Building

The new owner's first order of business is a fully rented building. Unfortunately, a common misconception in the residential real estate business is that a fully rented building means rents charged are too low. Traditionally, a property in the 95% to 97% occupancy range is considered stabilized and a good indicator of rates accepted by the market. Vacancy is used as a proxy for market rate rents. The cost structure of an apartment building, however, suggests it is in the owner's best interest to keep a fully rented building, even at lower rents.

The cost structure of a building has two components: fixed costs (FC) and variable costs (VC). The fixed costs are just that—fixed, and are borne by the building no matter how many units are rented. Fixed costs include property taxes and mortgage payments. Variable costs, however, change with the number of units rented. Variable costs include certain utilities and management fees, which generally increase with the number of units rented. Graphically, the difference between fixed costs and variable costs can be depicted as:

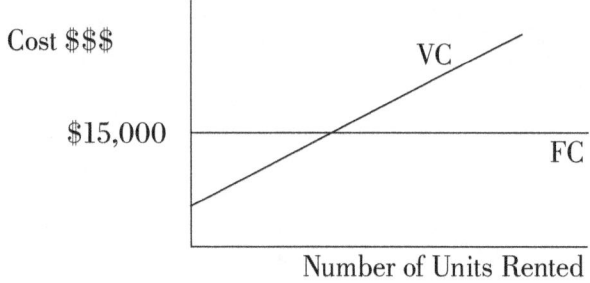

FC do *not* vary with the number of units rented. FC are shown as a horizontal line, in this example, at $15,000, whereas VC increase with the number of units rented.

Along with fixed costs and variable costs are a building's marginal cost (MC)— sometimes called incremental cost. The incremental cost is the increase in cost for the building that results from renting one more apartment. When one more unit is rented, there is a marginal cost, that little extra expense charged to the building.

But rental of one more unit is not all costs. On the other side of a rental is the marginal benefit (MB), defined as the additional rent generated by leasing one more apartment. Together, economics dictate the property owner should continue to rent apartments until the costs of renting one more apartment exceed the benefits of renting one more apartment:

Where $MB \leq MC$

The property owner should *stop* renting when the benefit of renting one more unit is less than the extra cost of one more rental, or where $MB \leq MC$, because the owner will lose money by renting one more unit. The corollary of this rule states the owner should *continue* renting as long as the additional benefit of renting one more unit is greater than the extra cost, or where $MB > MC$.

Take as an example the building discussed earlier with the initial proforma. Average rent in the building (one- and two-bedroom combined) was $500 per unit per month. $500 is the marginal benefit the owner receives per month by leasing one more apartment. Fixed costs include taxes, insurance, gas, electric (for the common areas), scavenger, and the mortgage. The property owner must bear these costs no matter how many units are rented. Fixed costs cannot be scaled down below a certain amount. By the same token, fixed costs do not increase as the number of units rented increases. Renting half the units, or all the units, does not require an increase in property taxes, insurance, utilities, or mortgage payments. But variable costs do increase with the number of units rented. For the building under study, variable costs are water, janitor, repairs, and management. These costs, per unit per month, from the initial proforma are the following(rounded):

Water	$ 8	($4,120/43 units/12 mos)
Janitor	$ 21	
Repair	$ 42	
Management	$ 21	
	$ 92	

Thus, the marginal benefit ($500) is clearly higher than the marginal cost ($92) the owner incurs for renting one more unit.

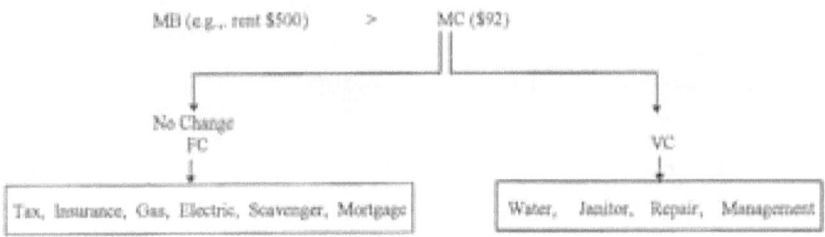

There is a substantial fixed cost component in operating the building. The building owner should continue renting available units at $500, $475, $450—in fact at any rent above $92—because, economically, the owner would be better off.

Many owners would recognize the opportunity cost created by renting a $500-unit at $93. The owner assumes the unit has a fair market rent of $500, and by renting the unit for less, the owner will be losing the opportunity to receive $500. Most owners will leave the apartment vacant a month or two (or longer in a less desirable neighborhood) until a renter comes along willing to pay $500 per month. Vacancy becomes the proxy for determining market rate rent—the monthly rent the unit will attract if kept on the market for a long enough period of time. But the investor's analysis is incomplete, as the discussion below reveals.

Assume a unit becomes vacant. Market rents are $490 to $500 for similar units in the area. By renting the apartment immediately for $475, the owner loses $25 per month the owner would have received if the owner held out for $500. Renting the unit at $475, the owner earns $5,700 ($475 x 12 months). If the owner waited a month for higher rent, the owner earns $5,500 for the same twelve-month period ($500 x 11 months + $0 vacant month). In this instance, the owner was better served by reducing the rent to $475 and earning $5,700 rather than $5,500.

Let us assume the property owner is dead set against reducing rent. Instead of reducing rent, the owner may alternatively offer one month free rent to entice renters and rent the unit more quickly. One month free rent has an advantage over reduced rent when the time comes to renew the tenant's lease. If rents increase 3%, from $500 to $515, the tenant is already psychologically committed to the higher rent, whereas an increase from $475 to $515 may be a real problem. But again, the owner must look at the cost of free rent against the cost of reduced rent with the *same* 3% increase:

Reduced rent: ($475 x 12 months) + ($490 x 12 months) = $11,580

One month free: ($500 x (12 months - 1 month free)) + ($515 x 12 months) = $11,680

In the final analysis, the owner is $100 better off with the free rent over a two-year period, not a significant influence on cash flow.

Vacant units are contrary to profit maximization. The property owner should not blindly assume if market rate rents are $500, that is what the owner should demand. Where a *large* portion of costs are fixed and, therefore, do not change with renting additional units, and variable costs are small, it makes sense to continue to rent as many units as possible to spread fixed costs. The concept of spreading fixed costs is not unique to real estate. Airlines apply the same concept to the sale of seats on a plane. As the time for the flight nears, airlines will sell empty seats on the plane for a reduced fare (in airline lingo, the airline increases its "load factor"—the ratio of passengers to available seats). The costs of flying the plane with a passenger in it are incrementally higher (fuel, food, beverage service), but the benefit to the airline, even with a reduced fare, far outweighs the marginal cost.

B

Paying Your Management Company Right

Once a property owner leases up the building, the owner's next concern is collecting all rents. Large apartment buildings require full-time property management. Even the small real estate entrepreneur with one or two buildings may not want to manage the properties full time and will have to hire others to help.

An owner's ability to create superior value in a property depends on the owner's experience using a stock of resources (property location, management experience, and know-how). Agency theory examines the use of financial incentives to motivate people to work harder.[1] In many situations, one individual, known as the principal, delegates responsibility to another, known as the agent, to act on the principal's behalf. How the agent acts will depend, in part, on how the agent gets compensated. Organizations do not necessarily get what they want, but they do get what they reward. Napoleon recruited volunteer armies by promising a share of the spoils—known today as incentive compensation. Owners now recognize the need to compensate management right.

Usually, the owner possesses an asset (the property) and employs management to increase its value. The terms of an agency relationship are spelled out by a management contract. The contract specifies the payments to be made by the owner to management contingent on management taking specific actions and the owner observing certain outcomes.

If the owner is unable to observe certain outcomes, an agency relationship may break down when management has an opportunity to "shirk." Shirking occurs because management may minimize efforts, working less hard than the owner would prefer. Consequently, the owner's goal is to maximize profits under a contract in which management will not shirk.

One key to prevent shirking is observability. If the owner has the potential to observe actions and outcomes, desired actions can be verified. For example, people who sell their house often require their sales agents to publish advertisements, host open houses, and show their home to as many prospective buyers as possible. Some actions of the agent may be harder to observe than others. In real estate selling, the owner cannot easily observe the sales pitch or marketing efforts used by the sales agent. For this reason, the owner is more likely to contract on a stipulated pay—commission—based on an observable outcome (the higher the sales price, the higher the commission).

If the property owner hires a management company, the owner ordinarily pays the outside management company a flat fee of 3.5% to 7% of revenues collected as a management fee.

Although a management company may be paid a straight percentage of revenues collected, say 5%, increasing on a straight line with revenues, the effort the management company must use to collect rents is not on a straight line. The reality may be 85% of rents will be collected without much effort. The tenants in this group generally pay rent on time and without additional steps by management. Another 10% of the tenants may need an occasional phone call or letter to be reminded to pay their rent. Depending on the neighborhood, the last 5% of tenants may be chronically in arrears and will need a demand letter by an attorney, five-day eviction notice or similar instrument informing the tenant they will be evicted for nonpayment of rent. Less than 1% of the tenants actually go to eviction.

These figures are not hard and fast but will change with the area, the building, and the market conditions. Whatever the exact figures, payment reflects the fact that the effort to collect the rent does not necessarily match the straight-line compensation usually paid to management.

The mismatch between compensation and effort is seen in the bottom line. Ownership wants all rents collected. Ownership makes its money in the last 5% of collections, whereas management may forego those 5% of rents that are the most effort to collect.

The 5% compensation paid to management works fine for 85%-95% of the rents, which management finds easier to collect, but not for the last 5% of rents, which may make the difference between profitability and loss, especially in the first few years of ownership. With straight-line compensation, the management company's compensation is not aligned with ownership's interests. The reality is that the management company is the owner's partner, but only for 5% of the collections. The misalignment between compensation and collection efforts is depicted in the following graphs:

To correct the problem, the property owner should not simply pay the management company more money, but should align the management's compensation with the effort required to collect the rents. If there is a one-to-one correspondence between compensation and effort, then contracting on compensation should induce the desired level of effort by the management company.

A three-tiered compensation system better aligns the management company's interests with those of the property owner than straight-line compensation. Graphically, the three-tiered compensation system mirrors the effort involved to collect the rents:

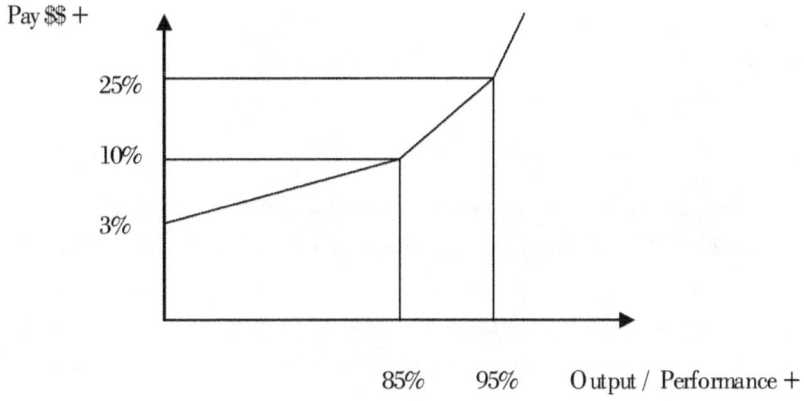

A substantial increase in compensation (3% to 10%, then 10% to 25%) matches the substantial increase in effort (Output / Performance). To see how the three-tiered compensation system works, assume—based on an actual building—collections averaged 95% of available rent, or $17,500 per month, which includes a 5% collection loss. But if collections were 100%, or 0% collection loss, the property owner would expect to receive, on average, $18,421 per month. The three-tiered compensation system could be broken down as this:

- 3% on collections less than $15,750 (85% of potential rents)
- 10% on collections between $15,750 and $17,500 (95% of potential rents)
- 25% on collection over $17,500 to $18,421 (the last 5% of potential rents)

Under straight-line 5% commission, the property owner was receiving an average of $17,500 per month and was paying the management company $875 ($17,500 x 5%). Under the three-tiered compensation system, however, the property owner would be paying only $648 for the same collections of $17,500 and $878 ($3 more than the $875) for 100% collections of $18,421. The management company would have more incentive to collect rents because the more they collect, the more they are paid:

Collections	% Compensation	Amount Paid Management
< $15,750	3%	$473
$15,750 - $17,500	10%	175
$17,500 - $18,421	25%	230
		$878

Remember, organizations get what they reward, not necessarily what they want. Under the three-tiered system, compensation is correlated with effort to maximize profits. The property owner seeks to align profit objectives with compensation for the management of the property. Ideally, the property owner wants the management company to feel like a part owner, committed to achieving the owner's profit goals through compensation that recognizes management's effort to achieve nearly 100% collections.

C

Getting Rid of Your Bad Tenants

Despite best efforts to fill a building with good tenants and collect rents, there will be, on occasion, a tenant who cannot, or will not, pay rent. Whether the decision not to pay rent is intentional (because there is a problem with the apartment) or unintentional (because the tenant lost a job), the result is the same: no rent. The property owner's local tax assessor, mortgage lender, and utility company expect payment on time. Creditors and extrinsic forces beyond the owner's control provide strong incentive for collecting all the rent the building can generate.

This section is in four parts: (1) rules of thumb for collecting of rent, (2) handling evictions, (3) screening tenants, and (4) employing a little-used remedy for landlords, the distress for rent.

1. Rules of Thumb for Collection of Rent

Property owners generally work with tenants having difficulty paying rent. After handling hundreds of evictions, a few rules of thumb may be helpful:

1. Find out the problem

2. Set firm deadlines
3. Act if the deadlines are not met

These rules are deceptively simple. Their usefulness depends less on the simplicity of the rules and more in their regular, consistent application.

First, find out the problem. Ask why the tenant is not paying rent. Eviction is usually the last resort. But in some cases, eviction may be the first resort if the tenant has simply decided to stop paying rent "Because," the landlord is told, "the rent is the other roommate's responsibility" or "I want to break my lease." Yet without knowing the problem, the landlord is unable to intelligently work with the tenant.

Second, get commitment from the tenant. Set firm deadlines. If the tenant expects to have the rent in a week, tell the tenant an eviction will be filed in ten days if the rent is not paid. The extra few days means if the rent is not paid, the landlord can move with a clean conscience and file an eviction by the deadline on the tenth day (sometimes called the "drop-dead date").

Third, act if the deadline is not met. Waiting is a big mistake. A tenant falls further behind in rent and eventually cannot pay the rent. By waiting, a landlord exacerbates a bad situation and loses credibility with other tenants, who will learn deadlines mean nothing.

Most landlords are unwilling to act because they are reluctant to acknowledge the loss and are overly optimistic the tenant will come through in the end. Landlords have a tendency to escalate commitment with a tenant. Landlords who commit themselves to a particular course of action (e.g., giving the tenant more time) make subsequent nonoptimal decisions (e.g., giving the tenant additional time) to justify their commitment to a previous decision (e.g., giving the tenant time to pay). Once the landlord makes an initial decision to give the tenant more time, negative feedback (the tenant still failed to pay) is dissonant with having made the decision in the first place.

One way to eliminate incongruity of thought (giving the tenant more time) with reality (but the tenant still failed to pay) is to escalate commitment to the initial decision by giving the tenant still more time in the belief that eventual success will now be achieved. The landlord engages in self-justification (if the tenant only had a little more time, payment would be made). To an outside observer, this way of thinking is dysfunctional and foolish.

To avoid the trap created by escalation of commitment, the landlord needs objective criteria to determine when to act. That criteria is simple—the landlord should file the eviction when the tenant was told the eviction would be filed. A machine-like process will avoid human decision errors that lead to escalation of commitment and a poor result.

2. Evictions

One area of life and legal relationships can truly be traced back over one thousand years: landlord-tenant relations. The lord received the land from the King and allowed serfs to live on and farm the land. Thus, we see the right of someone else—not the owner—to use and occupy the land with the owner's permission. In the Middle Ages, building structures were simple. There was no electricity or running water, so the tenant would make repairs for himself. In an agrarian economy, the land, rather than the building, was all-important. Over the centuries, English judges made decisions that created legal ideas known as the common law. As a result, in the present day, landlord-tenant relations are both historical and archaic in practice.

The average urban tenant of today has no interest in the land, only the three-dimensional space provided by the building. The law's important role of social ordering has followed the changing living patterns of its people. With increasing frequency, there has been a tendency by the courts to soften the harshness of the common law of property by applying contract principals to leases, imposing implied duties (meaning duties not specifically written into the lease but presumed to exist between the landlord and tenant) on the property owner based on a city's or municipality's building codes and ordinances.

In the last twenty-five years, comprehensive tenant laws broadly regulate the landlord-tenant relationship, not only as to possession of property, but also payment of rent, with a severe leaning toward consumer protection wherein the government cedes more of its responsibilities to private property owners who do not have the benefit of the government's police powers.

A last favorable remnant of the English common law that has been codified—that is, put into statute—is the property owner's right to evict a tenant for failing to pay rent. An eviction is a quick, simple, summary process by which *possession* of property is returned to the owner. A tenancy involves both a contract right and an interest in real estate (called a leasehold) which passes to the tenant from the property owner, giving the tenant the exclusive right to possess the real estate. The landlord retains a reversionary interest (simply a right to future enjoyment of property, at present in the possession of another) that will spring back to the landlord when the lease ends. Along with the right to possess the real estate through the leasehold interest, the tenant has the right of quiet enjoyment to use the property free from interference from the landlord and other persons. In exchange, the tenant must pay the landlord rent.

The tenant's obligation is pay rent is *contractual* in the lease, whereas the tenant's right to possession is a *property* right, which runs with the transfer of the leasehold interest from the landlord. The landlord-tenant relationship is defined both by contract and property law. Thus, a tenant's right to possession may terminate in an eviction, although the tenant's obligation to pay rent may continue until the lease ends.

Because the tenant's right to possession is a property right, a court must declare that right terminated. The property right, coupled with the more practical concern that a landlord's self-help eviction will lead to violence, require all evictions to go through a court process. Legally, an eviction constitutes a forcible entry. A forcible entry by anyone other than the law itself, in the body of the sheriff, is considered a breach of the public peace. A court order recognizes a tenant's right of possession has ended, and the court can thereupon order the sheriff to physically remove the tenant from the property.

The eviction process begins with a notice to the tenant that the tenant's right to *possession* will be terminated. The most common reason to terminate possession is the tenant's failure to pay rent. The notice usually gives the tenant time to cure the default, for example, by paying the back rent. If the default is not cured, the tenant's right to possession is terminated. When the tenant fails to leave, the law says the tenant is wrongfully detaining the property, and the landlord has a right to bring an action for forcible entry. Eviction cases are therefore more formally known as forcible entry and detainer actions. In short, a forcible entry and detainer has the purpose of adjudicating the right to possession (can the tenant stay or must the tenant go) and to prevent breaches of the peace (but landlord can't throw tenant out) by compelling aggrieved persons (the landlord and tenant) to assert their rights by peaceful means through the courts.

When the time comes to file an eviction, do so, and act. Do not escalate commitment that time and time again has shown only results in more losses. Follow the few rules of thumb: find out the problem, set firm deadlines, then act through the court system. These rules will minimize losses in the long run and ensure the property owner keeps good tenants who pay rent.

3. Screening Tenants

Evicting a tenant is one thing, getting payment for back rent is another. How can a property owner minimize losses and collect from a nonpaying tenant?

The first step is to be sure a tenant can pay rent in the first place. A tenant's ability to pay will be determined by proper tenant screening.

Any banker can explain the 3 Cs of lending: (1) credit, (2) collateral, and (3) character. With some modifications, the 3 Cs of lending can be used to measure the credit worthiness of tenants. The 3 Cs are like the popular metaphor of the three-legged stool. If one of the legs is missing, the stool is going to topple over. At the end of this book is a form rental application. There are dozens of forms, but all good ones ask for essentially the same in formation.

The first C, credit, means just that—what is the credit history of the potential tenant? Derived from the Latin meaning to rely, trust or believe, when a tenant gives credit, the tenant is asking the landlord to trust or believe the tenant will pay. A tenant's credibility, however, is better when corroborated with a credit report. For a small fee, credit brokers can obtain a credit report from the big three reporting agencies, Equifax, TransUnion, or Experian. The most important information will be any outstanding judgments, especially evictions (also known as UDs in some areas of the country for "unlawful detainer"). Evictions blackball a tenant with good reason. A tenant who has stiffed a landlord in the past will have a proclivity for stiffing landlords in the future.

A landlord may think a call to the tenant's current landlord will reveal problems. Not so. Tenants have been known to put down a friend as a landlord reference. Even if a tenant is truthful and gives a legitimate landlord reference, the current landlord may give a satisfactory report just to get rid of a bad tenant.

Bankruptcies are another bad mark, though the reason why is a mystery. Legally, a person who has gone through bankruptcy and received a discharge of debts cannot file for bankruptcy for another seven years. Thus, a tenant who filed bankruptcy two years ago is, first, relatively debt free having received a discharge of debts. Second, the tenant is prohibited from filing bankruptcy again for several years. Bankruptcy, therefore, will not be an immediate option to avoid payment of rent.

The second C, collateral, is more narrowly defined for a landlord than for a bank. A landlord should only be interested in liquid collateral, such as cash. Collateral for a tenant will mean (a) the security deposit, (b) tenant's wages, and (c) any bank accounts. With each of these, a judgment can be readily converted to cash and collected.

The third C, character, is the most subjective of the 3 Cs. Character means the tenant's truthfulness, accuracy, and thoroughness when asked to provide information. A potential tenant who puts down a false reference, the wrong social security number, an alias, or a different address every six months is not worth the potential problems.

4. Collecting Money Owed and Distress for Rent

Assume the landlord did everything reasonably possible, and the tenant still failed to pay rent. Reluctantly, the landlord sees no choice but to file an eviction. How can the property owner minimize losses and recoup back rent?

The property owner may join a claim for back rent with an eviction action in court. With a rent claim, a court will enter an order for eviction, and a judgment against the tenant for back rent. But a judgment does not mean automatic payment. A judgment is simply a judicial acknowledgment that money is due. The property owner will still have to collect the judgment. Collection involves an arcane process of bank garnishments, wage deduction orders, seizure of property, and sheriff levies. The judgment allows the property owner to call upon the court in aid of collecting the money owed. With a judgment, the property owner may use the police powers of the court to freeze property (assuming any can be found) and obtain an order directing a bank to turnover a bank account or an employer to withhold money from wages. In extreme cases, the police powers of the court may be used to effect the arrest of someone who failed to appear in court and disclose information about a tenant's assets that could be used to pay the judgment. Ultimately, all collections involve additional steps in a process that has already cost the property owner time, money, and aggravation.

Adding insult to injury, Congress has passed some pretty harsh laws that, although well-intentioned, impale honest people on technicalities. The Fair Debt Collection Practices Act, for example, generally requires a thirty-day notice period and limits a creditor's action to collect. This federal law is contrary to the intent of a quick and efficient process under a state's eviction laws. If a property owner does not follow the rules, the property owner may become the object of a claim by a tenant for a technical breach of the law and may wind up owing the tenant money.

Apart from legislation that affects a property owner's activities, property owners also face economic regulation in the form of taxes. Government protects property and redistributes wealth through taxes. The protection of property first appeared in a draft of the Declaration of Independence, where citizens could pursue life, liberty *and property*, rather than the phrase now known as "life, liberty, and the pursuit of happiness." The redistribution of wealth is achieved through the power of the government to tax. Taxes, cynics argue, collect income from one group of people and redistribute it to others in the form of government subsidies, aid, and welfare. Critics of this cynical view of government point instead to the many necessary services government provides. Consider streets, or a rapid transit system, surely these are unprofitable but necessary enterprises that only the government can furnish. Yet the cynics counter that government provides street and rapid transit to encourage growth in the inner cities, protect existing property, and allow people to commute to work, thus generating more taxable income.

Whatever role government plays, government and its laws affect a property owner's ability to collect back rent. Take bankruptcy as an example. A tenant who has not gone through bankruptcy in the last seven years always has that option. Bankruptcy is the final blow to an uncollected claim by discharging the debt and giving the tenant a fresh start. The U.S. Constitution, Article I, Section 8, recognizes bankruptcy; some say bankruptcy is a constitutional right not to pay debts.

What is a property owner to do? One remedy that is little used (probably because it appears draconian) is a distress for rent action. A distress for rent action is a self-help procedure. Similar to an innkeeper's lien, a distress for rent action allows a landlord to seize tenant property to cover back rent the landlord honestly believes is due. This self-help procedure must be performed by the landlord without a breach of the peace. This means the landlord should avoid a confrontation with the tenant and probably has to enter the apartment while the tenant is out during the day. It sounds like breaking and entering, but it is not—the landlord is exercising a lawful remedy.

Sometimes a landlord exercises a distress for rent action by changing the locks to the tenant's apartment. Lockouts are generally illegal. In Chicago, police have a standing order to arrest the landlord or property manager who fails to unlock an apartment. A few landlords have successfully argued that by changing the lock, they are exercising dominion and control over the tenant's property consistent with the distress for rent action.

The landlord must follow the law to be protected by the law. After seizing the tenant's property, the landlord prepares a list or inventory of the property taken. The inventory becomes part of the landlord's complaint for distress for rent and, in fact, may be attached to the one page form used as the "warrant" for distress for rent, i.e., the lawsuit that is filed with the court. It is also a good idea to post a copy of the distress warrant at the tenant's door. This notifies the tenant lawful action has been taken by the landlord.

The case may not be heard by a judge for several weeks. Before the case is heard, the tenant and the landlord would probably work out their differences because the tenant knows the rent is owed and wants the property back.

Distress for rent is seldom used. But when distress for rent works, it is successful because it is quick, immediate, and tangible—a tenant knows the landlord means business.

D

Keeping Your Good Tenants

The property owner now has a full building with 100% collections (most of the time). The owner's next concern is to minimize roll over and keep good, paying tenants as long as possible. This final section discusses (1) securing tenant commitment through incentives, cross-marketing techniques, and lease provisions that encourage tenant renewal, (2) tenant questionnaires, and (3) an impact matrix that allows the property owner to minimize market threats and maximize opportunities to increase a building's profitability.

1. Securing Commitment

The lifetime value of a loyal tenant can be astronomical—not only in terms of revenue, but in cost savings. Each time there is a rollover on an apartment, there is a vacancy loss (even if for only a brief period), advertising, apartment finder's fees, repainting and decorating, not to mention wear and tear on the common areas from tenants moving in and out. A property owner wants to keep tenants as long as possible, an operating philosophy of "lifelong" tenants.

Lifelong means five to ten years. A tenant typically stays a year or two then moves on. Imagine the savings, multiplied by *many units,* if tenants stayed for five or six years, even longer.

But how does a property owner get "lifelong" tenants? One way is to create tenant incentives for staying and disincentives for moving. Adopting an idea from the airlines, the property owner may use "frequent renter credits" akin to frequent flyer miles. After a tenant has a history of paying rent on time, the tenant accumulates credits toward free rent (days, weeks, or a month). Frequent renter credits may also take the form of tenant improvements. After a period of three years, a tenant who signs on for another year may chose an upgrade: a new kitchen (cabinets or appliances) or a new bathroom (vanity or tile). In this fashion, both sides to the transaction win. The tenant has an incentive to remain longer, now in an upgraded apartment, and the property owner benefits from tenant improvements for years to come that remain even after the tenant leaves. The tenant loses these credits if the tenant moves. The loss of credits is a switching cost, a penalty, thereby increasing the likelihood the tenant will stay so as to apply the credits earned.

Frequent renter credits also work with cross marketing. Ordinarily, a property owner with more than one building will transfer the security deposit from one building to the other, allowing the tenant to avoid the delay associated with the return of the deposit from the current landlord in order to pay the new landlord. With frequent renter credits, the property owner not only transfers the security deposit from one building to another but may transfer rent credits to the owner's other building.

The point is to make the incentives known and to make them systematic and predictable so tenants feel they have a vested interest in staying with current ownership. Participation leads to commitment. If tenants have an opportunity to take part in something, they have more interest in seeing it work. With the opportunity to participate in rent credits concerning their apartment, tenants will feel more committed to their rental decision.

Apart from incentives, the property owner should make it easy for tenants to pay rent. Curiously, some owners make it difficult for tenants to pay rent. Consider the owner who insists tenants deliver their rent payment by hand to the on-site property manager. Rent is delivered late; tenants complain they could not find the property manager or called the manager, who did not come until hours later or the next day, if they find the manager at all.

Rent is one of the largest consumer expenses a tenant has, generally representing 28% to 33% of a tenant's income. Tenants who pay late, or are in arrears with rent, force the property owner to act like a bank, carrying the unpaid rent for weeks, but usually without interest because of prohibitions in local landlord tenant ordinances (for example, the City of Chicago limits the amount a landlord may charge for late fees or interest). To encourage tenants to pay rent, a property owner may allow tenants to pay rent by credit card. The burden of collection then shifts from the property owner to the credit card company, which is better suited to act as a bank—in fact, is a bank—and loan money.

The property owner should also make it *easy* for tenants to renew their lease. Lease renewals typically involve management contacting tenants sixty to ninety days before the lease expires, sending a new lease and renewal forms to the tenants and chasing tenants to get signatures on lease renewals. At most, a lease may contain a provision, allowing the owner to show the apartment to prospective tenants ninety days prior to the lease expiration. Although this is a useful provision, there is probably no compulsion on behalf of any tenant to notify management sixty to ninety days in advance whether the lease will be renewed.

The lease can do more for the parties by providing for an *automatic* renewal of the lease (although local landlord-tenant ordinances may limit automatic renewal provisions, generally a well-drafted provision may work within these limitations). An automatic renewal clause will allow the lease to be renewed without any further action by the tenant or management:

> *Lease renewal.* Tenant must give written notice (the "notice") to management of tenant's intention not to renew the lease *at least 60 days prior* to the end of the lease. It is agreed the date of notice shall be the day the notice is received by management, not the date sent. Tenant understands if the notice is sent by mail, the notice may be received late and, therefore, the tenant should mail notice early, allowing at least a week for delivery. If the notice is not received as required, tenant agrees and acknowledges the lease will automatically renew for a one-year term with rent equal to 1.03 current rent.

A renewal clause allows the landlord to keep tenants with a built-in escalation of rent (here, at a 3% increase in rent). Some property owners prefer the old fashioned, more management intensive way of renewing each lease individually, providing better control over which tenant's leases are renewed. The perception of control is ephemeral. A lease with an automatic renewal clause may provide landlord control by simply stating: "Notwithstanding anything to the contrary in this lease, the landlord may terminate this lease by providing tenant sixty days notice of nonrenewal."

The automatic renewal clause has been challenged in court without much success. Tenants have argued the renewal clause was unfair or unconscionable because they missed the notice deadline and were stuck with the lease for another year. But courts find the automatic renewal fair because it was not unreasonable to require the tenant to notify the landlord in advance the apartment would be vacant and available for re-rental, giving the landlord time to market the unit. In fact, the Chicago Landlord Tenant Ordinance requires landlords to notify the tenant of an intent *not* to renew the lease because it is assumed the tenant would rather renew the lease than leave.

As a word of caution, some jurisdictions require the landlord to send a reminder to the tenant *before* the notice required in the automatic renewal clause. It may be a good idea to send a reminder even if the local law does not mandate it to avoid any surprise with the tenants.

The property owner should create incentives for tenants staying and disincentives for tenants leaving. Today's owners should be proactive, rather than reactive, anticipate tenants' needs, and use new ideas to secure tenant commitment.

2. Tenant Questionnaires

Questionnaires are another way to encourage tenant participation. If handled properly, questionnaires provide a forum for tenants. Questionnaires invite tenant participation. Tenant commitment to the property increases because tenants see someone is soliciting their opinion in order to make decisions about the housing that affects them. Questionnaires also provide direct systematic feedback for ownership.

Getting feedback directly from tenants may even provide more accurate information about a building's operation than information from management, who may selectively screen bad news.

Direct feedback from customers is used in many industries. Take, for example, Domino's Pizza. Fast delivery was Domino's strategic advantage in the market. For years, Domino's promised delivery within thirty minutes, or the pizza would be free. Domino's could have asked local stores to keep delivery records, but a store's self-reporting would be suspect. Instead, Domino's had their customers verify delivery times. Every free pizza meant the thirty-minute delivery time by the local store had not been met. Direct customer reporting provided Domino's headquarters with a more accurate measure of store delivery times than the stores would have themselves.

The idea of direct customer feedback can be carried over to real estate. A property owner may solicit tenant feedback using a questionnaire.

The tenants' feedback is demonstrated by the comments (discussed below) included in the following questionnaire used with a property:

You have been selected to answer questions about your apartment. We would like to know what you think about the building and what you would like to see improved. Your thoughts are important and will be kept strictly confidential. (Your name is optional.)

1. Do you get enough heat?

    ❏ Excellent   ❏ Good   ❏ Fair   ❏ Poor

2. How is security for the building?

    ❏ Excellent   ❏ Good   ❏ Fair   ❏ Poor

3. Extermination?

    ❏ Excellent   ❏ Good   ❏ Fair   ❏ Poor

4. When you have complaints, do you receive a prompt response?

    ❏ Excellent   ❏ Good   ❏ Fair   ❏ Poor

5. When you have a problem, do you receive courteous treatment?

   ☐ Excellent   ☐ Good   ☐ Fair   ☐ Poor

6. If you could pick only two items to remodel in the building, what would they be?

   ☐ bathroom   ☐ kitchen   ☐ windows
   ☐ appliances   ☐ fixtures   ☐ laundry room
                   ☐ other

7. If any of the improvements above were put in the building's budget, would you be willing to pay $XX a month more in rent?

   ☐ Yes   ☐ No

8. What do you like best about your apartment?
   _____
   _____

9. What do you least like about your apartment?
   _____
   _____

10. If we could improve our dealings with you, in what areas would that improvement occur?
    _____
    _____

OPTIONAL

_____
Name

Thank you for answering these questions. Please return your answers in the self-addressed stamped envelope provided.

The questionnaire had about a 35% response rate and provided both objective response questions and subjective commentary (question numbers 8, 9, and 10). Of those tenants who responded, a majority of tenants wanted improvements to the laundry room. Instead of spending limited money on other areas of the property, and new laundry room was built. The questionnaire also provided information about rents. Surprisingly, most tenants were willing to pay an increase in rent (answering yes to question no. 7), and one tenant even said, "I would actually pay even more than the increase suggested in the questionnaire." Most tenants also provided their name, even though their name was optional, demonstrating they wanted to share ideas with ownership.

With limited time and money, a questionnaire is a fast and inexpensive way to gather information. To keep tenant commitment, the property owner must follow up on tenant comments—perhaps by letter or a phone call to those tenants who identified themselves—and act in a positive, concrete manner to tenant suggestions. Most tenants would be willing to pay more and stay at a building if they see improvement—a visible, tangible manifestation the owner cares.

3. Impact Matrix: Threats and Opportunities[2]

Now that the property owner has found the right property, keeps it fully rented, with long-term paying tenants, the owner might wonder what else should be done to keep the property profitable. Here, the new property owner needs to step back to look at how the "business" of the property fits with the market around it. This section explores competitive advantages and argues to achieve them, a property owner must do a better job than its rivals at creating value. The ability to create value is shaped by how the property positions itself to compete in the market. The property must favorably distinguish itself from competitors in the eyes of the market place. The property owner has four areas of inquiry: (1) the mission statement, (2) the strategies used to fulfill the mission statement, (3) trends, and (4) constituent expectations, both of which are external forces that may impact the first two areas, mission and strategies, which are internal inquiries. We discuss each of these four areas of inquiry in turn.

1. *Mission Statement.* Returning to the mission statement at the beginning of this book ("to improve the properties we own, and to provide good housing at an affordable cost for as many people as possible"), the mission can be expressed by answering the following:

    a. *Whose needs* does the property appear to satisfy? (In the sample mission statement, ages 25-34, generally single, in the city area, of moderate income)
    b. *What needs* does the property appear to satisfy? (Housing)
    c. *What value* does the property provide for those needs? (Good housing at an affordable cost). The mission is the socioeconomic purpose of the property determined by tenant needs.

2. *Strategies.* Strategies are major decisions or programs employed by the property owner to fulfill the mission. Major decisions or programs mean the following:

    - they have far reaching consequences (long-term impact)
    - they are crucial to the survival and development of the property
    - they are broad in scope (affect a wide range of activities of the property)
    - they are difficult to reverse
    - they usually involve a significant commitment of resources

Consistent with the sample mission statement, strategies included major capital improvements ("to improve the properties we own"), building upkeep and maintenance ("to provide good housing"), and an aggressive acquisition program of housing ("for as many people as possible").

3. *Trends.* A trend is a basic underlying direction of development, a general tendency or course of events. A trend consists of the following:

    - an indication of direction (increasing or decreasing)
    - intensity of change (quickly or slowly)
    - relevant time horizon (days, weeks, months, years)
    - geographic dimension (neighborhood, local, city, statewide, national)

Trends include the aging of the nation's population (national, over years, slowly, increasing), or a growing Hispanic population (national with local focus, over years, slowly, increasing). Trends also include the shifting composition of households (unmarried people sharing an apartment or a single parent with children) and working at home (office space within the apartment, with upgraded electrical and phone lines to accommodate computers). Given the growing trend of working at home, a property owner may reconfigure space in the building, create an "office" in the apartment, or dedicate common space for an office, with a conference room, desks, and Internet access for those tenants willing to pay more. These trends suggest a movement toward larger units with extra space for an at-home office, day care within the property, and bilingual management personnel to address the needs of Hispanic tenants in major metropolitan areas.

4. *Constituents.* A constituent is an individual or group likely to be affected by the property. The constituent is also capable of taking action, which could impact favorably or unfavorably on the property. Constituents include tenants, investors, lenders, the neighborhood, city government, and property management.

Impact Matrix. The four areas of inquiry, (1) mission, (2) strategies, (3) trends, and (4) constituent groups, are an unwieldy mass of information. The property owner must develop a funneling process to assess market influences (trends and constituent demands) against the strategies and mission statement. An impact matrix allows a comparison of threats and opportunities and suggests change to the mission or strategies used to minimize a threat (-) or capitalize on an opportunity (+). The extreme positive or negative forces deserve managerial attention according to the following scale:

-3	-2	-1	0	+1	+2	+3
very high impact	force is a threat	low impact	stabilizing or has no relevance	low impact	opportunity	very high impact

The stabilizing forces (impact 0) are significant because any force which has a stabilizing effect implies the property owner's strategies and mission are in sync with external forces and, therefore, appropriate for the market.

To create the impact matrix, the property owner will disaggregate the mission statement into three parts in answer to the questions stated above: (1) whose needs are being served, (2) what needs are being served, and (3) what value is provided? The owner should identify three or four strategies, trends, and constituents, but may have more. First, going across the page (see impact matrix in the Appendix), the owner will assign a value to each box (-3 to +3) and add all positive forces and negative forces, placing a total (+) and (-) at the end of each row. Next, going down the page, the owner will add all positive and negative forces, placing a total (+) and (-) at the bottom of each column.

The values assigned in each box are admittedly subjective, but at a glance, allow the property owner to assess the interplay of the mission statement, strategies, trends, and constituent expectations. The highest and lowest values merit the owner's attention in three areas: (1) opportunity and threat to the mission, (2) opportunity and threat to strategy, and (3) opportunity and threat from external forces (trends and constituents). Once finished with the impact matrix, the property owner will determine whether change to the mission or a strategy is necessary, either because the mission or a strategy is threatened or because change would enable the property owner to exploit a new opportunity. In the example, the impact matrix offers the following observations:

Opportunity/Threat: Mission. In light of the trends and constituent expectations, a major mission opportunity in the market the property serves is "good housing at an affordable cost." (See Impact Matrix, Mission, "What Value", score 15). The owner may increase marketing along these lines, involve tenants and neighborhood groups, and even appeal to the City for assistance (government subsidies or programs). The owner is weakest in addressing the "whose needs" part of the mission statement and should question changing the mission or dropping this segment (25-34 age cohort, single, city, moderate income) as a target market in view of current trends. (See Impact Matrix, Mission, "Whose Needs", score -4).

Opportunity/Threat: Strategy. For strategy, a capital improvements campaign merits additional attention. (See Impact Matrix, Strategies, "Capital Improvements", score 20). Constituent groups such as the tenants, lenders, neighborhood groups, and the City expect strong performance in this area. On the other hand, the owner should consider modifying or dropping the aggressive acquisition program. (See Impact Matrix, Strategy, "Aggressive Acquisition", score -6). The aggressive acquisition strategy appears at odds with the core competencies the owner is attempting to develop in the mission.

Opportunity/Threat: External Forces (Trends and Constituents). Constituents, not trends, received the highest and lowest scores. Surprisingly, the neighborhood is the core constituency addressed by the mission statement, whereas the mission statement is ill suited for the investors' needs. If the owner wishes to appease investors, the mission and strategies should be changed. (See Impact Matrix, Constituents, "Neighborhood", score 14, "Investors", score -7).

Assuming the owner is concerned about investor needs, the owner may change the mission statement. For example, "To improve the properties we own, while at the same time reducing costs to find new and more efficient ways to operate." This mission statement may be better aligned with investor interests and an aggressive acquisition program. Through the acquisition of more buildings or a larger apartment building (one hundred units or more), the owner may fully exploit available economies of scale and spread fixed costs to operate more efficiently.

When a building is larger, the demand for certain services may become greater so the property will support specialists to handle work more efficiently. In lieu of using the building's janitor, the owner may hire specialists whose sole job is to handle specific maintenance, such as painting. Large buildings often have painters on staff. A full-time painter (or carpenter or plumber) will probably perform more efficiently, given more hours of practice and training, than a generalist who may perform certain work only occasionally. To reach economies of scale, the owner must have a larger or a greater number of properties so there are sufficient number of units to support the work of a specialist at the buildings. As the number of units increases, costs are averaged over greater volumes, tending to drive down costs. An aggressive acquisition strategy is better aligned with the mission statement which seeks "to reduce costs to find new and more efficient ways to operate" and will appease interests of investors as a constituent.

The impact matrix tests the appropriateness of the existing mission statement and strategies. Given the results of the analysis, the property owner may ask, What should the mission be? What should the strategies be? What needs should the property be satisfying? What tenants should the property be serving? If the answers are not what the owner expected, the mission and strategies may be misaligned and need changing.

End Notes

1. The following discussion is based on D. Besanko, D. Dranove and M. Shanley, *Economics of Strategy*, (1996), pp. 531-621, 633-35.
2. The following discussion is based on F. Neubauer and N. Solomon, "A Managerial Approach to Environmental Assessment," *Long Range Planning*, Vol. 10, April, 1977, pp. 1-8.

VII

CONCLUSION

It is said, if you do the things you have always done, you will always be where you have always been. It is important to try new things. Each person has the "right to try"; that within the framework of order, a person is by no means destined to do the same thing over and over again. If you do not try, you will never get your first deal. You should have the desire to carry out your first deal and begin at once.

Some people treat new information, such as the ideas discussed in this book, like a boomerang thrown in a midwinter blizzard. They know it is supposed to come back at sometime, but do not know how, when, or where. To avoid that situation, you should take the information in this book and make it your own. Then go out and try. Don't wait to close your next real estate deal.

APPENDIX

SAMPLE RIDER TO REAL ESTATE CONTRACT

RIDER TO REAL ESTATE SALE CONTRACT FOR
(ADDRESS, CITY, STATE)

I. *Conflict.* Should there be a conflict between the provisions of the real estate sale contract for (address, city, state) (the "contract") to which this rider to the contract (this "rider") is attached and the provisions of this rider, the provisions of this rider shall prevail.

II. *Documents to be furnished by owner*: Unless previously provided, within fourteen (14) days from the date of this agreement, seller shall furnish to purchaser, or make available to purchaser at a reasonable time and place for inspection, the following documents, lists, and schedules, which, together with any such documents previously delivered, are hereby certified by seller as being true, accurate, and complete:

   A. A current rent roll and any rent rolls in the last two (2) years, which include a list of all units of the building, the names of all tenants occupying each unit, the expiration dates of all leases, the rental for each unit, the names of any guarantors of the leases, the amount of advance rentals and security deposits received from each tenant, and all rentals which are in arrears; a current rent roll shall also be provided within forty-eight hours before closing.
   B. True and correct copies of all leases for any portion of the property (the "leases").
   C. All tenant credit files.
   D. All records of repairs or improvements made to the property since the seller's ownership of the property.
   E. True and correct copies of all management, leasing, maintenance, service, and other contracts, licenses, and equipment leases affecting the property (the "assigned contracts").
   F. A copy of the most recently paid tax bill for the property, or other document showing the amount of such bill.
   G. Seller's last two (2) year's Schedule E income tax returns for the property (seller may redact information unrelated to the property).
   H. A list of all persons employed by seller in connection with the management and maintenance of the property not disclosed in paragraph (E) above, which list shall show all compensation and benefits such persons may be entitled to receive.

III. *Inspection of property contingency*

   A. Seller shall permit purchaser and its agents, at reasonable times and upon reasonable advance notice to seller, to enter upon the property, at purchaser's sole cost and expense, for the purpose of conducting such physical inspections as purchaser may elect to make or obtain. Purchaser shall indemnify and hold seller harmless with respect to any damage to property or injuries to persons that may result from the inspections provided for in this paragraph, whether or not the transaction contemplated by this agreement closes.

B. Purchaser shall have a period of forty-five (45) days from the date hereof to notify seller in writing of any matter arising out of purchaser's investigation of the property pursuant to section II, and paragraph A of this section III. If the results of such investigations are not satisfactory to purchaser, or the property to be conveyed hereunder is not suitable for purchaser's intended use or purpose, purchaser may, on written notice to seller within such forty-five (45) day period, cancel the contract and this rider. If purchaser does not deliver a written notice of cancellation to seller within the forty-five (45) day period provided for above, the contingency provided for in this paragraph then shall be terminated.

IV. *Review of documents.* The contract and this rider are contingent upon seller's delivery to purchaser within fourteen (14) days from the date hereof of the documents and materials set forth in section II above. In the event that purchaser is not satisfied in its sole discretion with its review of the documents (or the documents are not produced or made available), purchaser shall have the right to cancel the contract and this rider.

V. *Contingency period.* Any money, earnest money, or deposit shall be held by for the benefit of both parties and shall be immediately returned or refunded to purchaser without further consent, authorization, or direction from seller upon written notice canceling the contract and this rider sent by purchaser within forty-five (45) days from the date hereof to seller or seller's attorney, and the seller hereby absolutely and irrevocably authorizes and consents to the return or refund mentioned in this paragraph without further consent, agreement, or authorization needed. If the purchaser does not send notice of cancellation within forty-five (45) days from the date hereof, the contingency period provided in this paragraph shall be deemed waived by the purchaser.

VI. *Seller's representations.* Seller represents to purchaser that the following matters are true as of the date of the execution of the contract and this rider (the "contract date") and shall be true as of the date of the closing of the transaction contemplated hereunder (the "closing date"):

A. *Title.* Seller is the legal fee simple titleholder of the property and has or will at closing have good, marketable, and insurable title to the property, and if a land trust is involved, seller represents that seller is the sole owner of the beneficial interest in the trust and has the authority to exercise the power of direction under the trust and is not subject to any restrictions on the exercise thereof. There are no judgments against the seller, there are no citation proceedings or other proceedings pending against the seller, which may be a charge or encumbrance against the beneficial interest in the trust.

B. *Physical condition.* There are no existing patent or latent physical defects or deficiencies in the condition of the property that would or could impair or impose costs upon the use, occupancy, or operation of the property that have not been fully corrected, and any improvements made by seller were completed and installed in accordance with all governmental authorities having jurisdiction thereover and do not violate any laws, ordinances, rules, or regulations.

C. *Utilities.* To the best of seller's knowledge, all water, sewer, gas, electric, telephone, drainage, and other utility equipment, facilities, and services for the property are installed and connected pursuant to valid permits, are adequate to service the property, and are in good operating condition and repair. Seller has not been notified of any condition that would or could result in the termination or impairment of the furnishing of service to the property of water, sewer, gas, electric, telephone, drainage, or other such utility services.

D. *Litigation.* There is no pending (or to the best of seller's knowledge, threatened) litigation, nor has there been any notice, complaint, or claim regarding the property of which seller is aware, nor are there proceedings in which seller is or may be a party by reason of any ownership or operation of the property, including building code, environmental, or zoning violations, or claims for personal injuries or property damage alleged to have occurred on the property, or, by reason of the condition, use of, or operations on, the property. No bankruptcy proceedings are pending, or to the best of seller's knowledge, threatened against seller, nor are any insolvency, bankruptcy, reorganization, or other proceedings contemplated by seller. In the event any of the foregoing is initiated or threatened prior to closing, seller shall promptly advise purchaser thereof in writing.

E. *Insurance.* Seller will maintain in force until the closing date casualty and liability insurance relating to the property and seller's assets to be conveyed hereunder. Seller has not received notice from any insurance carrier, nor is seller aware of any defects or inadequacies in the property that, if not corrected, could or would result in termination of insurance coverage or increase in the normal and customary cost.

F. *Personal property.* All personal property located in, on, or around the property to be conveyed by a bill of sale is in good and operable condition and repair and free of defects.

G. *Real estate taxes.* Seller has not received notice of and does not have any knowledge of any proposed increase in the assessed valuation of the property, or such other information, which would or could effect an increase in real estate taxes.

H. *Easements and other agreements.* Seller is not in default in complying with the terms and provisions of any of the covenants, conditions, restrictions, rights-of-way, or easements affecting the property.

I. *Environmental.* The property is now owned and operated in compliance with all state, federal and/or local environmental laws, regulations, and ordinances, including but not limited to the Resource Conservation and Recovery Act, the Comprehensive Environmental Response, Compensation, and Liability Act, the Illinois Environmental Protection Act, and all laws and regulations governing underground storage tanks, asbestos, and lead-based paints.

J. *Contracts.* There are no contracts of any kind relating to the management, leasing, operation, maintenance, or repair of the property, except the contracts delivered or furnished and made available to purchaser pursuant to this rider.

VII. *Additional conditions precedent to closing.* In addition to the other conditions enumerated in the contract and this rider, the following shall be additional conditions precedent to purchaser's obligation to close hereunder:

A. *Physical condition.* The physical condition of the property shall be substantially the same on the closing date as on the day of the contract date, reasonable wear and tear excepted.

B. *Real estate taxes.* As of the closing date, there shall have been no actual or pending reassessment of the value of the property for the purpose of calculating real estate taxes of which buyer has not been previously made aware.

C. *Utilities.* On the closing date, no moratorium or proceeding shall be pending or threatened affecting the availability, at regular rates and connection fees, of sewer, water, electric, gas, telephone, or other services or utilities servicing the property.

D. *Operation of property.* Seller shall continue to operate and manage the property in a first-class manner, maintaining present services, including pest control, and shall maintain the property in good repair and working order, doing such work as is necessary or advisable, and as would have

been done had the property not been placed under the contract and this rider for sale.
E. *Pre-Closing Expenses.* Seller has paid or will pay in full prior to closing all bills and invoices for labor, goods, material, and services relating to any alterations, installations, decorations, and other work for the period prior to the closing date. Except for those items for which purchaser has received a credit hereunder, purchaser has not agreed to, and will not assume, pay, perform, or otherwise discharge any debts, obligations, and liabilities of seller.

VIII. *Leases-Conditions Precedent and Representations With Respect Thereto*

Representations as to leases. With respect to each of the tenants (the "tenants") listed on the rent roll provided to purchaser by seller, seller represents to purchaser as follows, the ongoing truth of the following being a conditions precedent to purchaser's obligation to close:

A. Each of the leases is in full force and effect strictly according to the terms set forth therein and in the rent roll, and has not been modified, amended, or altered in writing or otherwise without notice to purchaser. Each tenant is legally required to pay all sums and perform all obligations set forth in the leases, without concessions, abatements, offsets, or other bases for relief or adjustment.
B. All obligations of the seller as lessor under the leases that accrue to the closing date have been performed including, but not limited to, all required tenant improvements, cash or other inducements, rent abatements or moratoria, installations, and construction (for which payment in full has been made in all cases), and each tenant has unconditionally accepted lessor's performance of such obligations. No tenant has asserted any offsets, defenses, or claims available against rent payable by it or other performance or obligations otherwise due from it under any lease.
C. No tenant is in default under or is in arrears in the payment of any sums or in the performance of any obligations required of it under its lease.
D. Seller has no reason to believe that any tenant is, or may become, unable or unwilling to perform any or all of its obligations under its lease, whether for financial or legal reasons or otherwise.
E. No guarantor(s) of any lease has been released or discharged, voluntarily or involuntarily or by operation of law, from any obligation under or in connection with any lease or any transaction related thereto.
F. There are no brokers' commissions, finders' fees, or other charges payable or to become payable to any third party not already disclosed on behalf

of seller as a result of or in connection with any lease or any transaction related thereto, including, but not limited to, any exercised or unexercised option(s) to expand or renew.

G. Each security deposit provided for under each lease shall be fully assigned to purchaser at the closing. No tenant or any other party has or has asserted any claim (other than for customary refund at the expiration of a lease) to all or any part of any security deposit.

IX. *Prorations and adjustments.* The following shall be prorated and adjusted between seller and purchaser as of the closing date:

A. The amount of all security and other tenant deposits and interest due thereon, if any, shall be credited to purchaser at closing. Thereafter, purchaser will be solely responsible for the security and tenant deposits, and purchaser agrees to indemnify and hold seller harmless from all claims by current tenants relating to the security and tenant deposits transferred to purchaser at closing.

B. Purchaser and seller shall divide the cost of any escrows hereunder equally between them.

C. Water, electricity, sewer, gas, telephone, and other utility charges based, to the extent practicable, on final meter readings and final invoices.

D. Amounts paid or payable under the assigned contracts shall be prorated.

E. All accrued general real estate taxes applicable to the property shall be prorated on the basis of 110% of the most currently available tax bills for the property. Prior to or at closing, seller shall pay or have paid all tax bills that are due and payable prior to or on the closing date and shall furnish evidence of such payment to purchaser and the title company.

F. Seller will pay the cost of the title policy, the survey, water and sewer certificates, all documentary and transfer charges relating to the instruments of conveyance contemplated herein. Purchaser will pay the entire cost of all documentary recording fees required by law relating to or concerning the instruments of conveyance contemplated herein.

G. Such other items that are customarily prorated in transactions of this nature shall be ratably prorated.

For purposes of calculating prorations, purchaser shall be deemed to be in title to the property, and therefore entitled to the income therefrom and responsible for the expenses thereof for the entire day upon which the closing occurs. All such prorations shall be made on the basis of the actual number of days of the year and month that shall have elapsed as of the closing date.

X. *Survival.* The representations, warranties, agreements, and covenants and indemnities of seller set forth in the contract and this rider shall remain in full force and effect regardless of any investigation made by or on behalf of purchaser and shall survive the closing and delivery of the deed pursuant to the contract and this rider.

XI. *Seller's closing deliveries.* At closing (or such other times as may be specified below), seller shall deliver or cause to be delivered to purchaser the following, in form and substance acceptable to purchaser:

   A. *Deed.* Seller will convey or cause to be conveyed to purchaser or its nominee title to the property by a recordable warranty deed, with release of homestead rights, if any, subject only to matters stated in the contract to which this rider is attached.
   B. *Bill of sale.* A bill of sale, executed by seller, assigning, conveying and warranting to the purchaser title to the personal property, free and clear of all encumbrances, other than the permitted exceptions.
   C. *Assignment of leases.* An assignment of the leases (including all security deposits and/or other deposits thereunder), in form and substance acceptable to purchaser.
   D. *Keys.* Keys to all locks located in the property.
   E. *Letters to tenants.* Letters executed by seller and, if applicable, its management agent, addressed to all tenants, in form approved by purchaser, notifying all tenants of the transfer of ownership and directing payment of all rents accruing on and after the closing date to be made to purchaser or at purchaser's direction.
   F. *Title policy.* If the title commitment or plat of survey discloses either unpermitted exceptions or survey matters that render the title unmarketable (herein referred to as "survey defects"), seller shall have twenty-one (21) days from the date of delivery thereof to have the exceptions removed from the commitment or to correct such survey defects or to have the title insurer commit to insure against loss or damage that may be occasioned by such exceptions or survey defects, and, in such event, the time of closing shall be thirty-five (35) days after delivery of the commitment. If seller fails to have the exceptions removed or correct any survey defects or, in the alternative, to obtain the commitment for title insurance specified above as to such exceptions or survey defects within the specified time, purchaser may terminate this contract or may elect, upon notice to seller within ten (10) days after the expiration of the twenty-one-day period, to take title as it then is with the right to deduct from the purchase price liens or encumbrances of a definite or ascertainable amount. If purchaser does

not so elect, the contract and this rider shall become null and void without further action of the parties.

G. *Original documents.* To the extent not previously delivered to purchaser, originals of the leases, the assigned contracts, assigned insurance policies, and governmental approvals.

H. *Closing statement.* A closing statement conforming to the proration and other relevant provisions of the contract and this rider.

I. *Plans and specifications.* All plans and specifications in seller's possession and control concerning the property and any improvements.

J. *Tax bills.* Copies of the most currently available tax bills.

K. *IRPTA.* An Illinois Responsible Party Transfer Act disclosure document, if and as required under Illinois law.

L. *Brokers' Lien Waivers.* Lien waivers of the brokers as required by the title company.

M. *Others.* Such other documents and instruments as may reasonably be required by purchaser (or its underwriters or lenders), its counsel or the title company and that may be necessary to consummate this transaction and to otherwise effect the agreements of the parties hereto. Notwithstanding any other provision of the contract, this subparagraph shall survive closing. After closing, seller shall execute and deliver to purchaser such further documents and instruments as purchaser shall reasonably request to effect this transaction and otherwise effect the agreements of the parties hereto.

XII. *Default.*

A. *Default by seller.* If any of seller's representations contained herein shall not be true or correct, or if seller shall have failed to perform, or failed to perform within the time for performance as specified herein (including seller's obligation to close), purchaser may elect either to (i) terminate purchaser's obligations under the contract and this rider by written notice to seller, and purchaser shall retain all rights and remedies available to it, including the right to a return of any money, deposit and/or consideration paid, or (ii) close, in which event purchaser may compel seller to cure any default(s). Purchaser shall be entitled to deduct from the purchase price or other amounts due seller the cost of any default that remains uncured. The remedies of purchaser set forth in this paragraph shall be in addition to remedies otherwise applicable or provided in the contract or this rider or otherwise available to purchaser at law or in equity. All time periods in this contract and rider shall be tolled upon any default by seller and shall not begin or resume running until such defaults have been fully cured.

B. *Default by purchaser.* In the event purchaser defaults in its obligations to close the purchase of the property, then seller's sole and exclusive remedy shall be to keep all money paid under the contract and this rider, the amount thereof being fixed as liquidated damages, it being understood that seller's actual damages in the event of such default are difficult to ascertain and that such proceeds represent the parties' best current estimate of such. Seller shall have no other remedy for any default by purchaser.

C. *Indemnity of purchaser.* Seller shall and does hereby indemnify, protect and hold purchaser harmless from and against any claims, losses, demands, liabilities, suits, costs, and damages, including consequential damages and attorneys' fees of purchaser and other costs of defense incurred, arising against, or suffered by purchaser or its assigns as a direct or indirect consequence of the following: (i) the breach of any representation or warranty of seller set forth in the contract or this rider; (ii) the failure of seller to perform any obligation required by the contract or this rider to be performed by seller, or (iii) any claims, costs, threatened or pending litigation arising from or relating to preclosing matters, including preclosing uses, operation or ownership of the property.

XIII. *Notices.* Any notice, demand, or request, which may be permitted, required, or desired to be given in connection herewith shall be given in writing and directed to seller and purchaser as follows:

Seller: _____

    Email/Fax _____

With a copy to seller's attorneys:_____

    Email/Fax _____

Purchaser: _____

    Email/Fax _____

Notices shall be deemed properly delivered and received (i) on the same day if personally delivered or delivered via facsimile or email, (ii) on the next day if delivered by Federal Express or other overnight courier, or (iii) on the third day after being deposited in the U.S. mail, regardless of actual date of receipt.

XIV. *Brokers.* Seller will indemnify, defend and hold purchaser harmless from and against any loss, damage, liability, or expense, including costs and attorneys' fees that purchaser may sustain as a result of any claim for a broker's commission, finder's fee, or other like payment in connection with this transaction, asserted by any person or entity who claims to have been employed by seller and who has not been previously disclosed to purchaser by seller. Seller hereby agrees to pay ("listing broker") consistent with the terms of the listing agreement between seller and listing broker, and the parties agree that, a licensed broker, shall receive X% of the purchase price as a commission to be applied by purchaser as a credit against the purchase price at closing. Purchaser will indemnify, protect, and defend seller as stated above in this paragraph from any and all claims by anyone who claims to have been employed by purchaser for a brokerage fee or the like.

XV. *Successors and assigns.* The contract and this rider shall be binding upon the parties' heirs, legal representatives, administrators, successors, and assigns, except that no party hereto may assign or transfer any of its interest hereunder without the express written consent of the other party.

XVI. *Miscellaneous*

    A. *Entire agreement.* The contract and this rider constitute the entire understanding between the parties with respect to the transaction contemplated herein, and all prior or contemporaneous oral agreements, understandings, representations, and statements are merged into the contract and this rider. Neither the contract and this rider nor any provisions hereof may be waived, modified, or amended except by an instrument in writing signed by the party against which the enforcement of such waiver, modification, or amendment is sought, and then only to the extent set forth in such instrument.

    B. *Time of the essence.* Time is of the essence of the contract and this rider.

    C. *Waiver.* No waiver by any party at any time of any breach of any provision of the contract and this rider shall be deemed a waiver of a breach of any of the provisions of the contract or this rider or a consent to any subsequent breach of the same or any other provisions.

    D. *Construction.* The contract and this rider shall not be construed more strictly against one party than against the other merely by virtue of the fact that it may have been prepared by counsel for one of the parties, it being recognized that both seller and purchaser have contributed substantially and materially to the preparation of the contract and this rider.

    E. *Governing law.* The contract and this rider shall be governed by and construed in accordance with the laws of the State of Illinois.

F. *Fax/Email.* The contract and this rider may be signed in counterparts with fax or electronic signatures and such shall constitute and be treated for all intents and purposes as an original document.

PURCHASER:

By: _____   _____
      Its Authorized Signatory   date

SELLER:

_____   _____
                                                   date
_____
Printed Name(s)

ADDENDUM TO REAL ESTATE SALE CONTRACT AND RIDER FOR [ADDRESS. CITY, STATE]

Seller Financing Contingency. The real estate sale contract and real estate sale contract rider for (address, city, state) is contingent on seller accepting a promissory note (the "note") in the amount of X% of the purchase price, secured by a second mortgage on the property. Purchaser shall have the absolute right to substitute collateral of equal or greater value for the second mortgage on the property before or after closing, and once collateral is substituted, seller agrees to immediately release the property from all liens, charges, and encumbrances relating to the note. The note shall be payable with interest at X% per annum, payable quarterly, to be amortized over XX years with a balloon payment as to the entire remaining balance not sooner paid upon sale or refinance of the property, or six (6) years. The note shall be fully assignable by seller without consent from purchaser.

PURCHASER:

By: _____   _____
      Its Authorized Signatory   date

SELLER:

_____   _____

_____   _____
Signature   date

SAMPLE TENANT APPLICATION

**YOU MUST PAY A $25 APPLICATION FEE.
2ND PERSON $15/EACH ADDITIONAL $10.**

**THIS FEE IS NOT REFUNDABLE UNDER ANY
CIRCUMSTANCES - NO EXCEPTION**

For Office Use Only	
Apartment Address	
Monthly Rent	Unit #
Move In Date	Security Deposit Amount

RENTAL APPLICATION

PLEASE TELL US ABOUT YOURSELF. EACH PERSON SHOULD FILL OUT A SEPARATE APPLICATION (This application takes approximately 5 minutes to complete)

1. Your Name: _____ _____ _____
   (First) (Middle) (Last)

2A. Your Work: _____ _____
   (Company Name) (Your Position)
   _____ _____
   (Address) (Phone Number)
   Contact/Your Supervisor: _____ _____
   (Name) (Phone Number)
   Your Salary: $_____ ☐ Hour ☐ Work ☐ Bi-Weekly ☐ Twice A Month (Check One)
   How Long Have You Worked There? _____ ☐ Yrs. _____ ☐ Mos.
   Any Other Income? $_____ ☐ Hour ☐ Work ☐ Bi-Weekly ☐ Twice A Month (Check One)

2B. Previous Employer: _____ _____
   (Company Name) (Your Position)
   _____
   (Address)
   Past Salary: $_____ ☐ Hour ☐ Work ☐ Bi-Weekly ☐ Twice A Month (Check One)
   How Long Did You Work There? _____ ☐ Yrs. _____ ☐ Mos.

3. Your Social Security Number: ☐☐☐-☐☐-☐☐☐☐
   Date of Birth: ___/___/___
   Mo. Day Year

4. Your Current Address: _____
   Phone Number Where You Can Be Reached: _____
   Landlord/Manager: _____ _____
   (Name) (Phone Number)
   How Long Have You Lived There: _____ ☐ Yrs. ☐ Mo. Current Rent: $_____

5. Bank Account: _____
   (Provide Bank Name)

6. WHO WILL LIVE IN THE APARTMENT WITH YOU? Please Include All Names. Only Those Named in This Application May Occupy The Apartment.
   (1) _____ (2) _____ (3) _____

7. HAVE YOU EVER BEEN EVICTED? IF YES, PLEASE TELL US WHEN AND WHAT HAPPENED. (We're more interested in learning about what happened, not to determine fault)
   _____
   _____

8. IMPORTANT - TWO PEOPLE WE SHOULD CONTACT IN CASE OF EMERGENCY:
   (1) _____ _____ _____ _____
       (Name) (Address) (Phone Number) (Relation)
   (2) _____ _____ _____ _____
       (Name) (Address) (Phone Number) (Relation)

**YOUR RENTAL APPLICATION WILL BE VERIFIED WITHIN 48 TO 72 HOURS
SHOULD YOU HAVE ANY QUESTIONS, PLEASE CALL (847) 382-5791 OR (630) 406-8851**

CONSENT AND CERTIFICATION

You agree we may rely on the information you gave us on your rental application. The information you have told us is true and complete. By signing this consent and certification, you agree we may ask others about you and your credit. We may also ask your employer about your salary, and you authorize your employer (and others) to release any information we request, including copies of recent pay stubs. As allowed by law from time to time, we may ask about your credit and employment. As long as you live at the property, this consent will be ongoing, and you agree we may get information about you and your credit.

Signature:_____

SSN:_____

CASE STUDY MATERIALS

Brochure

1st Letter of Intent

2nd Letter of Intent

3rd Letter of Intent

Post Inspection Letter to Seller

Post Contractual Modification Letter to Seller

[Broker Listing Sheet]
Chicago, Illinois

This forty-three-unit apartment building is located in the East Rogers Park Community on Chicago's Northside. The property is conveniently located near Lake Michigan, Rapid Transit, shopping areas, and schools.

INCOME/EXPENSE ANALYSIS

INCOME

RENTAL INCOME

6 units x 570.00/unit x 12	41,040	
36 units x 435.00/unit x 12	187,920	
1 unit x 350.00/unit x 12	4,200	
GROSS SCHEDULED INCOME	233,160	
VACANCY (%) 5%	11,658	
ADJUSTED GROSS INCOME		$221,502

EXPENSES

REAL ESTATE TAXES	44,921	
INSURANCE	5,235	
GAS	20,980	
ELECTRIC	2,360	
WATER & SEWER	4,020	
MAINTENANCE & REPAIRS	14,400	
JANITOR	15,000	
SCAVENGER	2,400	
MANAGEMENT (5%)	11,075	
MISCELLANEOUS & RESERVES	7,000	
TOTAL EXPENSES		$127,391
NET OPERATING INCOME		$ 94,111
CAPITALIZATION RATE	10.52%	
GROSS RENT MULTIPLIER	3.83	

Chicago, Illinois

General Description Forty-three-unit yellow brick courtyard building

Location	One block to lake, two blocks to El and bus, convenient shopping
Recent Improvements	New security fence and new security system
	Some entries and stairways retiled and painted, professionally landscaped, refinished exterior doors, newer hot water heater, all front stoops replaced, many apartments refurbished, including kitchens, bathrooms, paint, floors, stoves, and refrigerators
Apartments	Forty-three spacious apartments • 6 5 Rm 2 Bdrm 1 Bath • 36 4 Rm 1 Bdrm 1 Bath • 1 3 Rm 1 Bdrm 1 Bath
Terms	Cash, conventional, possible terms
Price	$895,000
Pin	xx-32-102-006
Taxes	$ 44,921
Price Per Unit	$ 20,814
Scheduled Gross	$221,502
Operating Expenses	$127,391
Net Operating Income	$ 94,111
Gross Rent Multiplier	3.83
Capitalization Rate	10.52%

[1st Letter of Intent]

June 21, XXXX

VIA. FACSIMILE

Dear

This letter is to advise you that [Purchaser] is willing to enter into negotiations concerning the eventual purchase of the above property on the following terms and conditions, it being understood that if Seller and Purchaser reach agreement on the terms of such a purchase, that agreement shall be memorialized in a written Contract.

1. *Property.* The property that is the subject of this letter is the land commonly known as [Address], Chicago, Illinois, and all buildings, improvements, and personal property thereon owned by Seller and located on and used in connection with the operation of the Property.
2. *Purchase Price.* The purchase price for the Property shall be $837,300.
3. *Seller Financing.* The Contract shall provide for Seller financing under which Purchaser shall pay Seller $50,000.00, and Seller shall take back a Note secured by a mortgage on the Property for the balance of the purchase price. The Note shall be an eight year balloon with a 40 year amortization, and shall carry an interest rate of 8.25%, 1.25% of which shall be deferred for the first two years following the Closing. Deferred interest shall be paid to Seller on the second anniversary of this Closing. Interest due under the Note shall otherwise be paid quarterly.
4. *Seller Tax Advantage.* The Purchaser is willing to structure this proposed transaction so as to minimize adverse tax consequences to the Seller (e.g., use of a lease with an option to buy to defer Seller's recognition of taxable gain, or a reverse amortizing mortgage).

5. *Real Estate Broker's Commission.* Purchaser and Seller hereby acknowledge [Purchaser's Principal] is involved in this transaction as a licensed broker and as such, is entitled to a broker's commission. As an inducement to Seller to consummate this proposed transaction, [Purchaser's Principal] will waive his cooperating broker's commission provided that [Listing Broker] agrees to pass along this savings to Seller by reducing its commission by the amount [Purchaser's Principal] would otherwise be entitled as a cooperating broker.
6. *Contract.* The parties and their respective attorneys will prepare and negotiate the Contract, based upon the terms and conditions in this letter, promptly after Seller notifies Purchaser that the terms of this letter are acceptable.

The purpose of this letter is to determine whether or not the parties are in sufficient accord as to the basic terms of the proposed transaction to warrant having the parties, together with their respective attorneys, draft and negotiate toward the execution of a definitive and binding Contract. This letter does not constitute the binding offer to purchase, and will not, upon execution by Seller, become a binding contract to purchase or sell the Property. It is specifically understood that no binding agreement or contract will be created unless and until the Contract referred to in paragraph 6 above is executed by both Purchaser and Seller. Notwithstanding the foregoing, Seller hereby agrees not to solicit, entertain or accept any formal or informal offers to purchase the Property (or an option to purchase the Property), or any part thereof, until both Purchaser and Seller have revoked this letter.

If the terms of this letter are acceptable to Seller, please inform the undersigned so that we may direct our attorneys to commence preparation of the Contract.

Very truly yours,

/s/_____

[2nd Letter of Intent]

July 3, XXXX

VIA FACSIMILE

Dear

[Purchaser] is willing to enter into negotiations concerning the purchase of [Address] Chicago, Illinois. The letter of intent dated June 21, is incorporated as part of this letter, but is changed in the following respects:

1. *Purchase Price.* The purchase price for the Property shall be $832,000.
2. *Seller Financing.* The Contract shall provide for Seller financing under which Purchaser shall pay Seller 10% of the Purchase Price, or $83,200 at closing, and Seller shall take back a Note secured by a mortgage on the Property for another 10% of the Purchase Price. The Note shall be payable with interest at 8.25% per annum beginning six months after the second year following closing, payable monthly, to be amortized over 30 years with a balloon payment as to the entire remaining balance not sooner paid upon sale of the Property, or eight years, whichever is first to occur.
3. *Conventional Financing.* The balance of 80% of the Purchase Price shall be paid to Seller at closing. Purchaser may obtain a loan from a bank or other source ("Lender") at a fixed rate of interest not to exceed 8.75% per annum, amortized over 30 years, payable monthly, with a loan fee not to exceed 1.5%. If such loan has a balloon payment, it shall be due no sooner than five years from closing. No private mortgage insurance shall be required by Lender.
4. *Real Estate Broker's Commission.* Purchaser and Seller hereby acknowledge that [Purchaser's Principal] is involved in this transaction as a licensed broker and as such, is entitled to a

broker's commission. [Purchaser's Principal's] commission may be applied at closing as a credit toward the down payment.

If the terms of this letter are acceptable to Seller, please let us know.

Very truly yours,

/s/_____

[3rd Letter of Intent]

July 12, XXXX

VIA FACSIMILE

Dear

[Purchaser] is willing to enter into negotiations concerning the purchase of [Address] Chicago, Illinois. This letter replaces our letter of July 3, XXXX. The letter of intent dated June 21, XXXX, is incorporated as part of this letter, but is changed in the following respects:

1. *Purchase Price.* The purchase price for the Property shall be $851,000.
2. *Seller Financing.* The Contract shall provide for Seller financing under which Purchaser shall pay Seller 10% of the Purchase Price, or $85,100 at closing, and Seller shall take back a Note secured by a mortgage on the Property for another 12.5% of the Purchase Price. The Note shall be payable with interest at 8.25% per annum beginning 24 months after closing, payable quarterly, to be amortized over 30 years with a balloon payment as to the entire remaining balance not sooner paid upon sale or refinance of the Property, or six years. The Note shall be fully assignable by Seller without notice or consent from Purchaser. Purchaser will provide Seller credit reports on Purchaser's principals from a major credit-reporting agency.
3. *Conventional Financing.* The balance of the Purchase Price shall be paid to Seller at closing. Purchaser may obtain a loan from a bank or other source ("Lender") at a fixed rate of interest not to exceed 8.75% per annum, amortized over 25 years, payable monthly, with a loan fee not to exceed 1.5%. No private mortgage insurance shall be required by Lender.
4. *Real Estate Broker's Commission.* Purchaser and Seller hereby acknowledge that [Purchaser's Principal] is involved in this transaction as a licensed broker and as such, is entitled to a

broker's commission. [Purchaser's Principal's] commission of 3% of purchase price may be applied at closing as a credit toward the down payment.

If the terms of this letter are acceptable to Seller, please let us know.

Very truly yours,

/s/_____

[Post Inspection Letter to Seller]

September 14, XXXX

*Sent Via Facsimile
and Original By Mail (with Confirmation of Fax)*

This notice is given to you pursuant to Paragraph V of the Rider to the Real Estate Contract dated August 7, XXXX providing for property inspection and a contingency period, which, by letter dated August 31, XXXX, was extended to September 14, XXXX. We have completed our inspection of records and of the Property, and are willing to purchase the Property subject to the following:

A. *Property Inspection*

You are invited to review the report provided by our property inspector, but generally, these facts were discovered during our inspection:

1. Approximately 6 apartments have holes in the ceilings or floors. Holes in ceilings were caused by a roof leak, or in one case, a leaky tub from the apartment above. Tenants informed us that you promised to repair many of these problems. We confirmed with the janitor, George, that you would effectuate repairs. (We also heard that all repairs were stayed pending the sale.) Under Paragraph VIII(2) of the Contract, the Sellers represented and warranted the ongoing truth of the following:

   All obligations of the Lessor under the Leases that accrue to the date of Closing have been performed including, but not limited to, *all required tenant improvements,* cash or other inducements, rent abatements or moratoria, *installations and construction* . . .

All required tenant improvements must be completed before Closing, or a credit given Purchaser at Closing.

2. Stoves are not functioning in about 12 apartments. Several other apartments are missing radiators. Paragraph VI in the second page of the Contract, Seller represented and warranted that:

> Seller represents and warrants that the *heating*, plumbing, electrical, central cooling, ventilating systems, *appliances and fixtures* on the premises are in working order and will be so at the time of closing, . . .

All appliances and radiators must be in place and operating before Closing, or a credit given Purchaser at Closing.

3. The building has a severe problem with rats and roaches. We saw dead rats, rat excrement and several live roaches. Tenants have complained to you. The building also has broken and open sewer lines. The tenants' complaints, rat and roach infestation, and broken and open sewer lines are a breach of Seller's representations and warranties contained in Paragraphs VI(B), (C), and (D). Paragraph VI(C) provides that all water, sewer and other utility equipment are installed properly and "are in good operating condition." In addition, Paragraph VI(B) provides:

> (B) To the best of Seller's knowledge, there are no patent or latent physical defects or deficiencies in the condition of the Property . . .

So too, under Paragraph VI(D), the Seller represented there have not been any complaints regarding building code violations, and under Paragraph VI(I), Seller represented the Property is being operated in compliance with all local ordinances. Rat and rodent infestation is a violation of Municipal Code §13-196-630. The broken and open sewer pipes are a violation of Municipal Code §13-168-120 and §13-196-610. The Property is simply not being operated in compliance with all local ordinances as represented.

4. Approximately 50% of the windows are missing screens, have broken screens, or are missing, or have broken, storm windows.

This is a violation of Municipal Code §13-196-560, and a breach of Paragraphs VI(B), (C), (D) and (I) of the Contract.

5. Holes on the roof are a violation of Municipal Code §13-196-530, and constitute a breach of Paragraphs 6, IV(B) and VI(I) of the Contract.

6. Our environmental consultant informed us that loose and friable asbestos exists on the piping in the boiler room and that this condition constitutes a health and safety hazard. Our consultant informed us that it will cost over $7,200 to remediate this asbestos contamination. In addition, our environmental consultant informed us that many of the apartments contain unremediated lead based paint. Our consultant informed us that it will cost approximately $4.25 per square foot to remediate this lead contamination. Paragraph VI(I) provides the Property is owned and operated:

> In compliance with all state, federal and/or environmental laws, regulations and ordinances, including but not limited to the Resource Conservation and Recovery Act, the Environmental Response, Compensation, and Liability Act, the Illinois Environmental Protection Act, and all laws and regulations governing underground storage tanks, asbestos, and lead-based paints.

The environmental defects at the property must be remediated before Closing, or a credit given Purchaser at Closing.

B. *Records Inspection*

1. We were disappointed to discover the repair and maintenance cost provided by [Seller's Broker] of $14,400 in the "Income/Expenses Analysis" was a theoretical figure. Nowhere on the Income/Expense Analysis were we told the $14,400 figure was an "estimate," an "approximation," or as [Seller's Broker] told us later, "pulled from the air." After reviewing Seller's records, the actual repair and maintenance expenses are twice the figure stated by [Seller's Broker]. The inaccuracy of the repair and maintenance cost is a breach of Paragraph II of the Contract, which provides

that the documents furnished by owner, "together with any such documents previously delivered, are hereby certified by owner as being true, accurate and complete." We detrimentally relied on the figures provided by [Seller's Broker] when deciding the value of the Property.
2. We have been unable to confirm the cost of the improvements made by the Seller. An itemization and specific records must be provided, and are required by the lender, to establish the representation and warranty made in Paragraph VI(B) of "a minimum of $100,000" in improvements.
3. The laundry room lease with A-N Parts and Service Co. is unacceptable. The Property must be sold free and clear of the laundry room lease.

In addition, there are other problems noted in the inspectors report that we can discuss by phone.

C. *Remedies*

The Purchaser has several remedies. The Contract provides:

> [I]f any of Seller's representations and warranties contained herein shall not be true or correct . . . Purchaser shall be entitled to deduct from the Purchase Price the cost of such action and cure, and all reasonable expenses incurred by Purchaser, including but not limited to, attorneys' fees of Purchaser.

(Contract, ¶XII(A)).

In addition, the Seller agreed to indemnify and hold Purchaser harmless:

> Seller shall and does hereby indemnify, protect, defend and hold Purchaser harmless from and against any claims, *losses*, demands, liabilities, suits, *costs* and damages, *including consequential damages* and attorneys' fees of Purchaser and other costs of defense, incurred, arising against or suffered by, Purchaser or its assigns *as a direct or indirect consequence of*:

(i) the breach of any representation or warranty of Seller set forth in the Contract . . .

(Contract, ¶XII(c)).

Accordingly, pursuant to the Contract, the Purchaser demands:

(A) The Seller cure the Seller's violations of warranties and representations under Paragraphs 6, VI(B), (C), (D), (I) and VIII(2) of the Contract; and
(B) The Seller credit Purchaser the amount of $55,000 against the Purchase Price for remaining uncured defects in violation of the Seller's warranties and representations; and
(C) The Seller extend the moratoria of interest and principal payments on Seller's financing for six years under the Note.

Sincerely,

/s/_____

[Post Contractual Modification Letter to Seller]

October 3, XXXX

VIA FACSIMILE

Dear

This letter modifies the contract dated August 7, XXXX, consistent with the parties' conversation on September 28, XXXX:

1. In exchange for the Seller providing:

    a. A dollar-for-dollar reduction in a purchase price to be applied as a credit against the Seller financing in the amount of $70,000; and
    b. The Seller agreeing to take back a promissory note in the amount of $36,375, or such greater amount as may be necessary given any difference between the original purchase price of $851,000 and the appraised value of the Property;

2. The Purchaser agrees to the following:

    a. Delete Paragraph 6 under page 2 of the Contract (Seller warranties and representations concerning the physical condition of the Property); and
    b. Delete Paragraph VI(B), (C), (D) and (I) to the extent these Paragraphs relate to physical condition or Seller representations and warranties concerning the physical condition of the Property; and
    c. Delete Paragraph X to the extent survival of warranties, representations, agreements, and covenants relate to, or touch upon the deleted Paragraphs; and
    d. Delete XII(C)(i) relating to the breach of any representation or warranty of Seller, with the exception of Warranty of Title under Paragraph VI(A); and

e. The Addendum to Rider shall be modified to reflect that the Seller financing shall be in the amount stated in Paragraph 1(b) above.

Sincerely,

/s/_____

AGREED:
/s/_____
Authorized Signatory for Seller

IMPACT MATRIX

IMPACT MATRIX

	STRATEGIES			MISSION			TOTAL IMPACT	
EXTERNAL FORCES FOR CHANGE / TRENDS	Upkeep and Maintenance	Capital Improvements	Aggressive Acquisition	Whose Needs: 25-34, single, city, moderate income	What Needs: housing	What Value: good housing at an affordable cost	Impact +	Impact -
Aging Population	3	3	0	-3	0	1	7	-3
Hispanic	-1	-1	3	2	0	2	7	-2
Single Parents, sharing	-1	-1	2	3	0	3	8	-2
Work at home	0	3	2	2	0	-1	8	-1
CONSTITUENTS								
Tenants	3	3	0	3	0	3	12	0
Investors	-1	-1	-3	-1	0	-1	0	-7
Landers	3	3	-3	0	0	-1	6	-4
Neighborhood	3	3	0	2	3	3	14	0
City	3	3	0	0	3	3	12	0
Management Personnel	1	2	0	1	0	3	7	0
Impact +	16	20	7	13	6	15		
Impact -	-3	-3	-6	-4	0	-3		

INDEX

3 Ps of negotiating 82
   preferences 61-2, 67-9, 72-7, 80-2
   preparation 75, 82
   priorities 22, 74-5, 77, 82, 124

A

absentee owner 26
active listening 62, 76-7, 82
   avoiding disruptors 76
   metadiscourse 76, 82
   silence 76-7, 82
age 40
agency theory 162
agent 162
aggressive acquisition strategy 185-6
amiable 64-6, 82
amortization 19
analytical 64-6, 82
apartment buildings 18, 21, 29, 38, 52, 157, 162, 185
articles of agreement for deed 122 *see also* installment sale contract
asking price 34-6, 42, 50, 77
at-home office 183
automatic renewal clause 177-8

B

bad debt 42-3, 46, 139
bankruptcy 107, 172-4, 197
broker 32, 70, 72-4, 95, 104, 127, 138-40, 142, 204
broker figures 138-9
buyer remedies 95, 114, 116-17, 119-20

C

C-corporation 128, 130-1
cap rate *see* capitalization rate
capital gains rate 19
capitalization rate 38, 40, 42, 47, 49, 215-16
cash flow 16, 38-41, 48-9, 52, 68, 71, 95, 97, 99, 101-2, 125, 141-2, 160
cash flow participation 71
character 171-2
Chicago Landlord Tenant Ordinance 178
collateral 71, 171-2, 205
commercial transactions 117
common law 169-70
complex analysis 30, 45, 47-8, 50-1, 57
compounding 143, 146, 149-51
constituent expectations 181, 184
contracts 12, 93-5, 104, 108, 116, 118-20, 143

breach of 94-5
default clause 114-15
due on sale clause 127
inspection clause 103
installment sale 120, 122-7
lease-option 120-2, 127
termination of 116
control 17, 19-20, 24, 26, 61, 65, 72, 75, 78, 109, 121, 167, 174, 178, 198
cost approach 39
cost structure 157
"cram down" position 140
credit 45, 140, 171, 176, 209
 loss of 176
credit files 97-9, 140, 195
credit report 171
credits, frequent renter 176
cross marketing 176

D

debt 34, 39, 71, 141, 144-5, 147
 cost of 143-9
debt hell 34
decision tree 62, 77-8, 82
Declaration of Independence 173
delayed closing techniques 120
denominator (costs) *see* denominator (expenses)
denominator (expenses) 22
depreciation 18-19, 39, 56, 123, 130
discount rate 40, 48-9
disincentives 176, 178
distributive negotiations 80
dividend payments 16
documentary intermediary 72
double taxation 130
drop dead date 168

E

earnest money 103-5, 116, 127, 141, 196
Equifax 171
equity 18-19, 115, 144-5, 147-8
EV *see* expected value
evictions, handling of 167
expenses 18, 21-3, 35, 39, 43-4, 51, 89, 95, 97, 99, 102-3, 112, 115, 123-4, 127
external obsolescence 31, 56
externalities 56
extrovert 64-5, 82

F

failure to close 116
Fair Debt Collection Practices Act 173
FC *see* fixed costs
financing 32, 56, 63, 68-72, 80, 93, 116, 120, 131-2, 139-42, 147, 205, 219, 221, 229
fixed costs, spreading of 157, 160
Florida factor 32, 137
forcible entry 170-1
formula for future worth of 16
functional obsolescence 39, 56

G

GRM *see* gross rent multiplier
gross rent 137, 215
gross rent multiplier 39, 137, 215-16

I

IDEA 18-19, 21
illiquidity 16-17, 34
 de facto status of 16
 premium 16
impact matrix 175, 181, 183-6, 231-2
"to improve the properties we own" 24, 182, 185

incentive compensation   162
income   11, 18-19, 43
income capitalization approach   38-9
incremental cost   158
indemnity   115, 117
inferential conclusion   76
information   17, 25-6, 29, 35-6, 62-3, 65-6, 75-7, 95, 97-9, 102, 139, 171-3, 179, 181, 209
initial proforma   42-5, 47, 138, 158-9
initial yield   38, 40, 145
inquiry, four areas of   181, 183
inspection   97-8, 102-6, 114, 116, 118-20, 140, 195-6, 223
insurance   43-4, 46, 107-8, 110, 117-18, 123, 138, 142-3, 158-9, 197, 201-2, 215
Integrative Negotiations   62, 79, 81
interests, types of   131
intermediary   12, 17, 62, 68, 72-4, 82, 93
internal rate of return   48
Internal Revenue Service   18
IRR *see* internal rate of return
IRS *see* Internal Revenue Service
"as is" condition   143

J

joint tenants   129
judgment   172
   collection of   172

K

knowledge
   general   26
   specific   25-6

L

land trust   106, 128-9, 196
land trustee   129
landlord-tenant ordinances   177
landlord-tenant relations   169
lease   41, 52, 121, 177
   with an option to buy   120-1, 124
   renewal of   52, 177
   residential   52
leasehold   170
lender scrutiny   148
leverage   17, 22, 141-4, 147-8
leverage-based efficiency gains   22
lifelong tenants   175-6
limited liability   128, 130-1
Limited Liability Company (or LLC)   130
limited partners   130
liquid collateral   172
"livery of seisin"   93
load factor   160
loan covenants   132, 148

M

marker rate rents   157
master lease   121
MC *see* marginal cost
mission statement   24-5, 181-6
month-to-month tenants   41
mortgage
   interest-only   71
   sliding   71
   standstill   71
   walk the   71
multipreference negotiations   81

N

neighborhood   15, 31-2, 41-2, 49, 52, 54, 56, 139, 159, 163, 182-5, 232
net income   38
Net Operating Income   38-40, 42, 44-7, 49, 145, 215-16
NOI *see* net operating income
numerator (income)   22-3
numerator (income) growth   22-3

O

one-issue negotiations 80
one-way negotiating 73
operating agreement 130
operating expenses 39, 42-4, 46, 123, 138, 141, 145, 216
ordinary gain rate 19
out-of-control property 26
ownership 12, 15, 31, 37, 45, 47, 50, 56, 93-4, 98, 107, 117, 128-31, 141-2, 164

P

partnership 72, 128-31
  termination of 131
payment 19, 50, 71, 100, 104, 112, 118, 123-5, 129-30, 139, 146, 167-9, 171-2, 199-201, 204-5
physical and economic vacancy 42 *see also* bad debt
physical deterioration 18, 39, 56
poor man's financing 120
poor negotiators 76
position 68, 76, 113, 117, 140, 143
pragmatic 64-5, 82
price anchoring 33-6
price/earnings ratio 39
principal 162
productivity ratios 22
professional analyst 17
profit 12, 15-16, 18, 21, 23, 34, 91, 93, 141-2, 160, 166
property
  motivation to own 15
  physical inspection of 102
  profitability of 21-2
  right 12, 29, 31, 34, 93, 170, 181
  value of 34, 36, 38
property ownership *see* real estate ownership
prorations 69, 111-12, 119-20, 200, 202
purchase price 29, 39-40, 45, 50-1, 68-70, 104-5, 115-16, 120-2, 124-5, 139-42, 204-5, 217, 219, 221-2, 226-8

R

real estate 11-12, 15-19, 21, 23-6, 34-5, 37, 54, 57, 61-3, 95, 108-9, 120-1, 128, 130-1, 198
  investment 16, 19, 57
  negotiations 61-3
  ownership 15, 128
  residential 15, 54, 155, 157
  selling of 163
  tax reproration agreement 113
  transfer of 93
Real Estate Sale Agreement 95
reciprocity 81
rent 177
  collection of 41, 164-5, 167, 177
  losses 99, 165
  distress for 167, 172, 174
rent credits 120-2, 176
rent roll 42, 97-100, 195, 199
repairs, record of 99
replacement reserve 44
residual participation 71
return on asset 144-5, 148
return on equity 144-5, 147
return strategies 16
revenue growth 23-4
reversionary interest 170
RIDER to REAL ESTATE SALE CONTRACT 195
ROE *see* return on equity
Roosevelt, Franklin Delano 15

S

S-corporation 128, 130-1
Sales (or Market) Comparison Approach 39
seller financing 32, 56, 63, 69-72, 80, 116, 131, 139-42, 147, 205, 217, 219, 221, 228-9
Seller Representations and Warranties 99, 105-6, 108-9, 114, 118, 120, 142
seller's tax returns 97, 99
service-profit chain 23
setoff 116
shirking 163
silent partners 130
skilled negotiations 75
sophisticated investors 117
stalemate 79-80, 82
stock, "holding" of 16
stock investing 16
stock market 16-17, 35, 39
straight-line compensation 163-5
straight sale 120
strategic sense 68
strike price 121-2

T

tax break 18
tenant incentives 176
tenants 11-12, 22-4, 52-3, 129, 182-5
  getting rid of bad tenants 167-70, 174
  issues 41-2
  keeping good tenants 175, 181
  questionnaires 155, 175, 178
  screening of 167, 171
  securing commitment of 175
tenants in common 129
threat, minimization of 183
three-tiered compensation system 165
three-tiered system 166
time 16, 19, 42, 48, 64, 69, 71, 115, 120-2, 162, 168, 170, 173, 178-9, 181-2
title insurance policy 143
"on top" of the property 25
transfer costs 25
TransUnion 171
trends 181-5, 232

U

undervalued common stocks 17
"undervalued" real estate 17
unlawful detainer (UD)

V

value-redistributing effects 94
variable costs 157-60
VC *see* variable costs

www.ingramcontent.com/pod-product-compliance
Lightning Source LLC
Chambersburg PA
CBHW021358210526
45463CB00001B/138